The CELPIP General Study Guide

Complete Review & Test Prep With 170+ Exam Style Practice Questions & Answers

Written by Fred Winstone

© *Copyright of Fred Winstone 2025*

Table of Contents

About the Book 4

Introduction 7

Chapter 1 – Listening 17

Chapter 2 – Reading 47

Chapter 3 – Writing 79

Chapter 4 – Speaking 109

Chapter 5 – Practice Test Questions & Answers 157

   CELPIP Mock Test 1 – Full Questions 161

   CELPIP Mock Test 1 – Answers 195

   CELPIP Mock Test 2 – Full Questions 204

   CELPIP Mock Test 2 – Answers 237

Conclusion 247

About the Book

If you're reading this, chances are you're planning a new chapter in your life—maybe you're applying for permanent residency, Canadian citizenship, or need to prove your English skills for work or school. Whatever your goal, this is an important step that needs to be conquered, and this book has been written with that in mind.

Preparing for an English language test can feel overwhelming. You may be juggling work, family, or studies while trying to find time to study. You might feel nervous about your speaking or writing skills, or unsure about what the test will be like. This book has been designed to be a clear, supportive guide that makes the process easier, less stressful, and more manageable.

The CELPIP (Canadian English Language Proficiency Index Program) Test is designed to measure how well you use English in everyday situations—not just in a classroom, but in real life.

You'll be asked to demonstrate how you communicate effectively in various settings, including at work, with friends, in your community, and through written materials such as emails or notices. That means you don't need to sound perfect; you just need to show you can function confidently and clearly in English.

This book focuses on the **CELPIP – General Test**, which:

- Assesses all four language skills: listening, reading, writing, and speaking.
- Is completed in just one test sitting—about 3 hours total—so there's no need to come back for a separate speaking test.
- Is officially approved by Immigration, Refugees and Citizenship Canada (IRCC) for Permanent Residency applications.
- Is also recognized by many universities, colleges, and professional associations across Canada.

In these pages, we will go through everything you need to know: what to expect, how to prepare, and how to approach each part of the test. You'll find real-world examples, helpful tips, and strategies that make sense. The goal is to help you feel confident, capable, and ready, not just for the test, but for life in an English-speaking environment.

You've already taken the first step by deciding to prepare—and that says a lot about your determination. So, take your time, be kind to yourself, and remember that progress happens one step at a time.

Introduction

"The beautiful thing about learning is that no one can take it away from you." - **B.B. King.**

If you picked up this book, you're probably preparing for one of the most important moments of your life—taking the CELPIP Test. Whether your goal is permanent residency, citizenship, career advancement, or personal growth, you're in the right place. Let me reassure you: you are *absolutely* making the right choice.

You see, there's something powerful about knowing you've taken control of your future. That's exactly what you're doing right now by committing to this guide. You want to feel prepared, confident, and ready. And this book is here to deliver exactly that.

Getting Started with This Guide

Preparing for a test like CELPIP can feel overwhelming. Maybe you're unfamiliar with the test format. Maybe English isn't your first language, and you're unsure where to even begin. Or perhaps, like many others, you're under a lot of pressure—whether from tight immigration deadlines, work goals, or family responsibilities.

This guide is designed to remove that uncertainty. It provides everything you need: strategies, sample responses, practice questions, clear explanations, and insider tips that have helped others succeed—and they will help you too.

Why You Can Trust This Guide

I've spent years helping English learners build confidence, master communication skills, and successfully prepare for English proficiency exams. I've worked with students from all walks of life—newcomers to Canada, professionals seeking better opportunities, and families hoping to build a future here. I understand how this test works, and more importantly, I know how to teach it.

This book isn't theory. It's practical, proven, and written from experience. I've poured all my knowledge into this guide with one goal in mind: to help you succeed.

What You Will Gain from This Book

By the time you finish this book, you will:
- Understand the CELPIP test format, timing, and scoring

- Feel confident in all four test areas: Listening, Reading, Writing, and Speaking
- Learn strategies that help you think like a top scorer
- Practice with realistic sample questions and model responses
- Know exactly what to expect on test day
- Feel fully prepared to reach your target score

Real Results, Real People

Maria, a nurse from the Philippines, was overwhelmed and did not know how to improve in the speaking section of the CELPIP examination. After looking for as many resources as she could, she came across this book and started practicing by using the sample responses for each section. She passed her CELPIP exam with the score she needed for her permanent residency.

"When I was preparing for the CELPIP exam, I felt overwhelmed, especially with the speaking section. I didn't know how to improve or where to start. After searching through countless resources, I finally found this book. The sample responses and clear structure helped me practice with confidence. Thanks to this guide, I

passed the CELPIP with the score I needed for my permanent residency!"

— *Maria S., Registered Nurse*

She's not the only one. Hundreds of students have used these exact techniques to transform their preparation and achieve success. And you can, too.

The Promise

This book is not a magic wand. But if you commit to reading it and applying what you learn, you will feel more confident and prepared than ever before. You will understand the test, feel in control, and give yourself the best possible chance of achieving your goals.

The promise is simple: if you follow the guidance in this book, you will be ready.

Why You Should Start Now

CELPIP is more than just a test. For many, it's a gateway to a better life: a new job, a new country, a new beginning. Every day you wait is a day further from your goal. But every day you study, practice, and grow brings you closer. You can take charge of your future starting today. So, with that, let's get started and take the first step toward your CELPIP success!

Understanding the CELPIP Test Format

The CELPIP General Test is designed to measure your ability to use English in everyday situations. It covers:

- **Listening**: Understanding spoken English in conversations and discussions.
- **Reading**: Understanding written passages, advertisements, emails, and more.
- **Writing**: Composing emails and survey responses.
- **Speaking**: Responding to prompts and situations using a microphone.

Test Duration and Scoring

The test is completed in one sitting and takes about **3 hours**. Each component is scored from 1 to 12, with scores aligned to the Canadian Language Benchmarks (CLB).

For many immigration and citizenship applications, a CLB level of 7 or higher is often required.

Essential Test Information

- **Test Locations**: CELPIP is available both online and at more than 140 test centers in Canada as well as globally. You can find locations online.

- **Registration**: Register online at CELPIP Registration
- **Fees**: $290 CAD + tax (Canadian pricing; international may vary)
- **Test Day Requirements**: Bring a valid photo ID and your confirmation email.
- **Retaking the Test**: You can retake the test as many times as needed, provided there is a minimum of 4 calendar days between attempts.

Transfers and Cancellations

Transfer Policy

If you need to reschedule your CELPIP Test:

- **Eligibility:** You can transfer to another test session of the same type (e.g., CELPIP-General to CELPIP-General).
- **Timing:**
  - **At least 7 calendar days before** the original test date: You can transfer your test through your CELPIP Account.
  - **Less than 7 calendar days before** the test: Contact Paragon's customer service at 778-327-6854 or info@cael.ca. Paragon may require supporting documentation

(e.g., a doctor's note or evidence of bereavement) to process the transfer.

- **Fees:**
  - **First transfer:** Free of charge.
  - **Subsequent transfers:** CAD 50 plus applicable taxes.
- **Process:**
  - Sign in to your CELPIP Account.
  - Under "Upcoming test," click "Actions," then select "Transfer to a different sitting."
  - Follow the prompts to complete the transfer.

Note: Transfers are subject to availability and must be for the same test type.

Cancellation Policy

If you are unable to attend your scheduled test session:

- **Timing:**
  - **At least 7 calendar days before** the test date: You may cancel your registration through your CELPIP Account.

- o **Less than 7 calendar days before** the test date: You may still cancel, but no refund will be provided
- **Refunds:**
  - o **At least 7 days before:** You will receive a refund of 50% of the test fee.
  - o **Less than 7 days before:** No refund will be issued.
- **Process:**
  - o Sign in to your CELPIP Account.
  - o Navigate to your test registration and select the cancellation option.
  - o Follow the instructions to complete the cancellation.

Note: Cancellations are only processed through your CELPIP Account and must adhere to the specified timelines.

Retake Policy

If you wish to retake the CELPIP Test:

- **Frequency:** You may register for only one test session within any 5-calendar-day period. Registrations violating this rule may be canceled by Paragon.

- **Preparation:** It is recommended that you engage in additional study before retaking the test. CELPIP provides various study materials and resources to support your preparation.

Note: Ensure that your test registrations comply with the 5-day interval policy to avoid cancellations.

For more detailed information or to manage your test registration, please visit the official CELPIP Policies & Forms page.

https://www.celpip.ca/take-celpip/policies-forms/

How to Use This Book Effectively

This book is organized in a step-by-step manner to guide you through each section of the CELPIP test. In it, you will find:

- Strategies to help you tackle each question type
- Sample questions with explanations
- Model answers for writing and speaking tasks
- A test-day checklist to ensure you're fully prepared

Study Tips

- Create a study schedule that fits your routine.
- Focus on your weaker areas first, but don't ignore your strengths.
- Use the practice questions to simulate real test conditions.

This is your roadmap to CELPIP success. You don't have to guess your way through preparation. Let this book serve as your guide, coach, and study partner.

Your future starts now.

Chapter 1 – Listening

"Most people do not listen with the intent to understand; they listen with the intent to reply."
– **Stephen R. Covey**

Overview

The Listening component of the CELPIP (Canadian English Language Proficiency Index Program) test is designed to assess your ability to comprehend spoken English in a variety of real-world contexts.

This section of the test reflects the kinds of conversations, announcements, and discussions you may encounter in daily life in Canada, whether at work, in public spaces, or during social interactions. It evaluates your ability to understand the general meaning, identify specific information, and interpret implied ideas based on spoken language.

The goal of this section is not just to test your ability to recognize English words, but to assess how effectively you can follow and respond to information that is presented through speech.

This includes understanding tone, attitude, and purpose, as well as making inferences and drawing conclusions from what you hear.

Test-takers are expected to listen carefully and respond to a variety of question types that assess different listening skills. You might hear a conversation between coworkers solving a problem, a customer asking for help in a store, or a radio announcer presenting a news report. Each task is designed to replicate everyday listening situations in Canada, ensuring that your English comprehension skills are practical and applicable.

Overall, this part of the CELPIP test is a vital measure of how well you understand spoken English, and it plays a significant role in determining your readiness to function effectively in an English-speaking environment like Canada.

As you move through the different sections, you'll be tested on your ability to follow conversations, identify important details, understand instructions, and evaluate opinions, all of which are essential skills for successful communication in everyday life.

Format, Structure, Scoring, and Time Limits

The Listening section is structured into six parts, beginning with one unscored practice task. This initial task is provided to help you become familiar with the test format, audio delivery, and the types of questions you will encounter.

Following the practice task are six scored components that cover a range of listening scenarios, each with its own specific focus and set of questions. The entire Listening section takes approximately 47 to 55 minutes to complete.

The Listening section of the CELPIP test follows a clear and structured format, designed to evaluate various listening skills through different types of spoken content. Understanding the format ahead of time can help you manage your time wisely and prepare more effectively for each task.

- **Total Duration:** 47–55 minutes
- **Total Number of Questions:** 39

The Listening section is divided into the following parts:

Section	Number of Questions
Practice Task	1
Part 1: Listening to Problem Solving	8
Part 2: Listening to a Daily Life Conversation	5
Part 3: Listening for Information	6
Part 4: Listening to a News Item	5
Part 5: Listening to a Discussion	8
Part 6: Listening to Viewpoints	6

Because the entire Listening section is timed, and because the audio cannot be replayed, it is essential to stay focused and manage your time efficiently throughout the test. Taking brief notes during the recordings can help you recall key details when answering the questions.

Types of Listening Tasks

Part 1: Listening to Problem Solving

What to Expect:

Here, you will listen to a conversation between two people who are working together to find a solution to a shared problem. The situations are usually practical and reflect everyday life, such as planning an event, making a purchase, or deciding on an activity. The goal is to test how well you can understand the process of problem-solving as it happens in natural conversation.

The dialogue typically follows a logical sequence, beginning with the identification of a problem and then proceeding to a discussion of possible solutions. You will hear the speakers share their opinions, weigh the pros and cons of each option, make suggestions, and eventually come to a decision.

What You'll Hear:

You will hear two people engaged in a discussion where they explore different options. Their tone is usually friendly and conversational. The conversation may include polite disagreements, compromises, and reasons behind their choices. Phrases that signal decision-making or preference are common, such as:

- "What if we try...?"

- "That might work."
- "I don't really like that idea."
- "Let's go with..."
- "That sounds like a good plan."

These expressions can help you understand how the speakers are narrowing down their choices and moving toward a solution.

Question Format:

There are 8 multiple-choice questions in this section. Each question is based on the content of the conversation you just heard. The questions will ask about the main problem, the solutions discussed, the speakers' preferences, and the final decision, if one is made. You may also be asked to infer the reason behind a speaker's suggestion or to understand how one speaker responds to another.

Tips to Approach This Section:

- **Focus on the main problem.** As the conversation begins, try to clearly identify what the speakers are trying to solve. This will help you follow the discussion more easily.

- **Track the options discussed.** Pay attention to each suggestion the speakers make and what reasons they give for accepting or rejecting them.

- **Listen for agreement or disagreement.** Words and tone will often indicate whether a speaker likes or dislikes an idea.

- **Note the final decision.** If the speakers agree on a solution, make sure you catch what it is, as this may be directly asked in one of the questions.

- **Use context clues.** Even if you're not sure about every word, the overall tone, vocabulary, and structure of the conversation can help guide your understanding.

- **Listen for signal phrases.** Common decision-making phrases include "Maybe we should...", "That's not a bad idea," and "I'd rather not do that."

Example Scenario

Two university students, Maya and Josh, are working on a group project for their marketing class. They meet up at the campus café to figure out how to divide the work.

Maya: "So, the project's due in two weeks. I don't mind doing the research and writing up the report. That's kind of my thing."

> **Josh:** "Perfect! I actually enjoy designing slides and talking, so I'm happy to handle the presentation part."
>
> **Maya:** "Awesome. Should we set a deadline for the research part? Maybe next Monday?"
>
> **Josh:** "Yeah, that works. Then I can start putting the visuals together after that. Let's also check in on Friday, just to make sure we're both on track?"
>
> **Maya:** "Sounds like a plan."

The questions in Part 1 will reflect your ability to understand the situation, the choices discussed, and the reasoning behind the final outcome.

Part 2: Listening to a Daily Life Conversation

What to Expect:

In this section, you will listen to a short, informal conversation that reflects everyday interactions. The scenarios are drawn from common, real-life situations you might experience while living or working in an English-speaking environment. The purpose of this section is to evaluate your ability to understand casual, conversational English in typical day-to-day settings.

The conversation typically involves two people, such as friends, coworkers, family members, or service providers, discussing a routine topic. These conversations are often straightforward and direct, but they can also include subtle details or emotional cues that are crucial for answering the questions.

What You'll Hear:

You will hear a relaxed and natural exchange between two speakers. The tone can be friendly, neutral, or occasionally slightly formal, depending on the relationship between the speakers.

The topics are familiar and relatable, such as discussing plans, confirming appointments, making purchases, or catching up with someone after some time.

Some examples of conversation topics include:

- Booking or rescheduling an appointment
- Asking for directions
- Discussing a recent event
- Making a casual request
- Shopping or returning a product

Because the tone of voice and specific words used can reveal how the speakers feel or what they intend, paying attention to how something is said is just as important as what is being said.

Question Format:

This section includes **5 multiple-choice questions** that are directly based on the content of the conversation. The questions may ask you about:

- Specific details (e.g., time, date, place)
- The relationship between the speakers
- The reason for the conversation
- The outcome or plan agreed upon
- Emotions or attitudes expressed by one or both speakers

Tips to Approach This Section:

- **Pay attention to tone and emotion.** The way someone speaks can reveal a great deal about their emotions. For example, a cheerful tone may indicate satisfaction, while a hesitant tone could suggest uncertainty.

- **Listen for details.** Small factual elements, such as when an appointment is scheduled or where someone is going, often appear in the questions. Jotting down key details as you listen can be a helpful strategy.

- **Understand the purpose of the conversation.** Try to quickly grasp why the speakers are talking. Is one person requesting help? Are they sharing news? Identifying the main purpose can guide your understanding of the rest of the dialogue.

- **Focus on relationships.**
Understanding how the speakers know each other can provide useful context. Is this a customer and a receptionist? Two colleagues? A parent and child? Clues may come from the language they use or how formal they are.

- **Anticipate next steps.** Some questions will ask what the speakers decided or plan to do next. Pay attention to the end of the conversation to catch this information.

Example Scenario

Sarah calls her dentist's office to reschedule an upcoming appointment. The receptionist, Lisa, picks up the phone.

Lisa: "Good morning, Dr. Patel's office. This is Lisa speaking—how can I help you?"

Sarah: "Hi Lisa, it's Sarah Jacobs. I have an appointment next Tuesday, but something's come up and I need to reschedule."

> **Lisa:** "No problem at all. Let me pull up your file... Okay, I see it here. We've got some openings later that week—would Thursday morning work for you?"
>
> **Sarah:** "Hmm, I've got a meeting then. Do you have anything in the afternoon?"
>
> **Lisa:** "Let's see... How about Thursday at 3:30?"
>
> **Sarah:** "That works perfectly. Thanks so much!"
>
> **Lisa:** "You're all set for Thursday at 3:30. We'll see you then!"

This kind of task prepares you for practical listening in everyday situations. Understanding the details and dynamics of simple conversations is essential not only for the test but also for real-world interactions in English-speaking environments.

Part 3: Listening for Information

What to Expect:

In this section, you will listen to a monologue, meaning one person speaking without interruption. The speaker typically provides practical, organized information in settings such as a workplace, a guided tour, or a public announcement. This section assesses your ability to comprehend structured spoken information that you may encounter in everyday life in Canada.

The purpose of this part is to evaluate how well you can follow explanations, instructions, or descriptions and identify the key details presented. The language is clear and purposeful, and the speaker often follows a logical sequence to present the information effectively.

What You'll Hear:

You will hear a single speaker delivering information in a calm, steady tone. The content is informative and may include explanations, overviews, or step-by-step instructions. This could be a guide explaining points of interest during a tour, a supervisor outlining tasks for the day, or an announcer providing information about an event or service.

The speaker typically uses transition words and phrases—like "first," "next," "after that," and "finally"—to organize their ideas. These cues help you follow the structure and locate the most important points.

Common features of this section include:

- A clear introduction and conclusion
- Factual details (such as dates, times, locations, or quantities)

- Organized delivery of information
- Occasional comparisons or emphasis on specific points

Question Format:

This section contains **6 multiple-choice questions**, all based on the content of the talk. The questions may ask you about:

- The main purpose or topic of the speech
- Specific details such as names, times, or instructions
- The sequence of events or steps
- The structure of the information
- What the listener is expected to do with the information (e.g., follow directions, remember key points, complete a task)

Tips to Approach This Section:

- **Identify the main idea.** Listen carefully to the beginning of the talk to understand its content. This helps you organize the rest of the information in your mind.
- **Take note of specific facts.** Numbers, names, dates, and other data are often tested. Jotting these down as you listen can help you answer questions more accurately.

- **Pay attention to transitions and sequence.** Words like "first," "then," and "afterward" show the order in which things happen or are explained. These markers can help you understand the structure of the talk and follow along more easily.

- **Listen for emphasis.** The speaker may slow down, repeat a point, or use phrases like "what's important to remember is..." to highlight key ideas.

- **Stay focused throughout.** Because the speaker talks continuously without interruption, it's essential to stay engaged the entire time so you don't miss critical information.

> **Example Scenario:**
>
> A team leader is giving a short introduction to a new employee about the office layout and how things work.
>
> **Team Leader:**
>
> "Hi! Welcome to the team—we're really glad to have you on board. Let me give you a quick overview of the office so you can get settled in.
>
> Your desk is just down this hallway on the left, near the windows. The kitchen and break area are right around the corner—you'll find coffee,

> tea, and a fridge there if you want to store your lunch.
>
> Meeting rooms are along the back wall, and each one is labeled, so they're easy to find. If you ever need to book one, just use the calendar system on your computer.
>
> Now, if you need help with anything technical, IT is in Room 204—a super helpful team. And HR is just upstairs if you have questions about benefits or schedules.
>
> I'd also recommend checking out our internal site later today—it has links to all the tools and resources we use on a daily basis.
>
> Take your time getting settled and let me know if you need anything."

This part of the test helps assess your ability to absorb spoken information in situations where you are expected to listen carefully and understand without needing to ask questions. Mastering this skill is essential for functioning independently in many real-life settings, from following workplace instructions to understanding public service announcements.

Part 4: Listening to a News Item

In this section of the Listening test, you will hear a brief news report presented by a single speaker.

The content is similar to what you might hear on the radio, a podcast, or a television broadcast. It typically covers a recent local or national event and includes factual information about what happened, who was involved, and why it matters.

Your task is to understand the key details of the story and the overall message. This section assesses your ability to follow current event-style content, which is relevant to everyday life in Canada and helps demonstrate your understanding of informative spoken English.

What You'll Hear:

You'll listen to a single speaker, such as a news anchor or journalist, delivering a concise report. The tone is usually neutral, clear, and professional. The speaker will describe an event or situation using facts, often accompanied by supporting data, such as numbers or quotes from those involved.

Typical features of the audio include:

- A headline or main topic introduced at the beginning
- Background context to explain why the story is important
- Key facts such as dates, locations, and people involved

- Consequences or reactions to the event
- A logical flow, with clear cause-and-effect relationships

The report is usually structured to give you the essential facts quickly and effectively, and it may include updates or ongoing developments.

Question Format:

This part includes **5 multiple-choice questions**. These questions test your comprehension of:

- The main idea of the report
- Specific details, such as who was involved, what occurred, or when it happened
- The purpose of the report (e.g., to inform, to raise awareness)
- Impacts or results of the event
- Causal relationships, such as what caused the event or what happened as a result

Tips to Approach This Section:

- **Focus on the 5Ws and 1H** (Who, What, Where, When, Why, and How). These are the core elements of any news report and will help you locate the most relevant information quickly.

- **Listen for cause and effect.** News stories often explain why something happened and what the outcome was. Paying attention to these relationships can help you answer questions about implications or consequences.

- **Pay attention to numbers and names.** If the speaker mentions statistics, dates, or specific people or organizations, take note. These are commonly tested details.

- **Consider the purpose of the report.** Ask yourself: Is the speaker simply informing, alerting the public to a situation, or providing an update? Understanding the intent can help you choose the correct answer when options are close in meaning.

- **Stay alert to structure.** News stories typically start with the most important information and then provide details. This can help you anticipate what kind of information might come next.

Example Scenario:

A weather forecaster on Canadian radio gives a detailed update on the week's weather. The forecast begins with a summary of current

> conditions and what listeners can expect for the day.
>
> The forecaster then outlines the weather outlook for the rest of the week, highlighting temperature changes, chances of rain or snow, and any weather alerts in effect. They provide details specific to different regions, such as coastal winds in British Columbia or cold fronts moving through Ontario.
>
> The report may include comments from Environment Canada and advice for commuters or outdoor workers. The forecaster might also mention seasonal trends and how this week's weather compares to averages for this time of year.

This part of the CELPIP Listening section mirrors real-life situations where understanding news reports is important for staying informed about your community and the broader world. Being able to listen critically, pick out relevant facts, and understand the structure of a news item will help you succeed in this section and build confidence in your overall English comprehension skills.

Part 5: Listening to a Discussion

In this section of the Listening test, you will hear a group discussion, usually involving at least three speakers who are working together on a shared topic, task, or project. The conversation is collaborative, and the speakers exchange ideas, opinions, and suggestions.

This part of the test is designed to assess how well you understand multiple speakers as they interact naturally, as you might experience in a workplace, study group, or volunteer meeting in real life.

What You'll Hear:

The audio will feature multiple viewpoints, with each speaker contributing their thoughts and responding to others. The discussion may involve decision-making, brainstorming, problem-solving, or evaluating different options. You'll hear a range of opinions, suggestions, agreements, disagreements, and potential compromises as the group works toward a common goal.

As you listen, pay attention to:

- The flow of conversation—how each speaker takes turns and builds on or challenges ideas
- Tone and language, which can reveal attitudes, preferences, and priorities
- The overall direction of the discussion and any final decisions made

The dialogue is realistic, meaning it may include casual language, overlapping speech, or changes in topic, much like a real conversation with multiple people.

Question Format:

This part includes **8 multiple-choice questions**. These questions are based on different aspects of the discussion, including:

- The main topic and purpose of the conversation
- Each speaker's viewpoint or suggestion
- Agreements and disagreements between participants
- Any decisions or conclusions the group reaches
- The reasons behind certain suggestions or preferences

You will need to carefully identify who says what and understand how the speakers respond to each other throughout the discussion.

Tips to Approach This Section:

1. **Listen actively to each speaker.** Try to distinguish their voices and note their individual opinions and suggestions.

2. **Keep track of different perspectives.** Write down brief notes about what each person thinks or proposes—it will help when answering questions.

3. **Pay attention to reactions.** Look out for verbal cues that show whether someone agrees or disagrees, such as "That's a good point," or "I'm not sure about that."

4. **Identify a compromise or resolution.** Discussions often end with a decision or mutual understanding. Make note of what conclusion, if any, is reached.

5. **Be alert for transitions.** Speakers may shift topics or reconsider their opinions based on others' input. Follow these changes closely.

Example Scenario:

At a school meeting, the principal addresses a group of parents about plans to improve student engagement and community involvement.

The principal begins by welcoming everyone and thanking them for attending. She then outlines two main ideas the school is considering: starting a weekend reading program to support literacy and organizing a monthly family volunteer day to strengthen school-community connections.

> Some parents express enthusiasm about the reading program, especially for younger students. Others are more interested in the volunteer initiative and ask how it would be scheduled and managed. The principal listens to their input, addresses questions about staffing and funding, and explains how each option supports the school's goals.
>
> After discussing the pros and cons, the principal invites parents to complete a short survey to help guide the decision. She emphasizes the importance of collaboration and promises to follow up with the final plan in the coming weeks.

This section assesses your ability to follow group interactions, a crucial communication skill in many real-life settings. By identifying individual opinions, tracking group dynamics, and understanding how decisions are made, you will be better prepared to engage in collaborative environments and perform well in this part of the CELPIP Listening test.

Part 6: Listening to Viewpoints

In this final part of the Listening section, you will hear a single speaker presenting their opinion or viewpoint on a particular issue. Unlike conversations or discussions, this is a monologue—meaning just one person speaking—where the speaker clearly expresses their thoughts and feelings about a subject. Your goal is to carefully listen and understand not only what the speaker thinks but also how they support their ideas and what attitude or emotion they convey. This section tests your ability to comprehend persuasive or explanatory speech, which is common in everyday life, media, and workplace communications.

What You'll Hear:

You will listen to a speaker who shares a clear point of view, often related to a social topic, workplace policy, or community issue. The speech is usually organized logically, with the speaker presenting a main argument, followed by reasons, examples, or evidence to support their opinion. The speaker's tone can vary—it might be passionate, enthusiastic, concerned, or calm—giving you important clues about their attitude toward the topic.

Question Format:

This part consists of **6 multiple-choice questions** that focus on different aspects of the monologue, including:

- The main idea or argument expressed by the speaker

- The supporting reasons or evidence given to back up the opinion

- The speaker's tone and attitude (e.g., whether they sound excited, worried, or neutral)

- How the speaker organizes their points and builds their case

- Any conclusions or recommendations the speaker makes

To answer these questions correctly, you will need to pay close attention to both the content and the way it is delivered.

Tips to Approach This Section:

1. **Focus on the main argument.** Identify the speaker's overall opinion early on and keep it in mind throughout the listening.

2. **Listen for supporting details.** Notice examples, facts, or explanations the speaker uses to strengthen their viewpoint.

3. **Pay attention to tone and emotion.** The speaker's feelings about the issue can help you understand their perspective more deeply.

4. **Follow the structure of the speech.** Look for phrases like "Firstly," "In addition," or "Finally," which signal how ideas are organized.

5. **Avoid distractions from minor details.** Concentrate on the key points and how they relate to the speaker's opinion.

Example Scenario:

At a staff meeting, an employee discusses the benefits of implementing a wellness program within the company.

They explain that a wellness program could include activities like regular fitness classes, mental health workshops, and healthier snack options in the break room. The speaker highlights how such initiatives can reduce stress, improve employee morale, and lower healthcare costs.

They also mention that encouraging wellness shows the company cares about its employees' well-being, which can boost loyalty and reduce turnover. The tone throughout the speech is upbeat and convincing, aiming to persuade management and coworkers that investing in wellness is a smart move for everyone.

This section challenges your ability to understand persuasive speech, which is common in news, presentations, and everyday conversations where someone clearly expresses their opinion.

By identifying the main ideas, supporting details, and tone, you will be well-prepared to answer questions accurately and demonstrate strong listening comprehension skills on the CELPIP test.

Listening Tips to Help You Succeed

- **Practice Active Listening**

    Engage fully with the audio—don't just hear it, *listen* with focus. Try watching English shows or news with subtitles, then without.

- **Familiarize Yourself with Accents**

    CELPIP uses Canadian accents but may include others. Practice listening to different English accents online.

- **Improve Notetaking**

    Jot down keywords, not full sentences. Capture names, numbers, places, and important ideas.

- **Understand Question Types**

    Know what each question is testing—main idea, specific detail, inference, attitude, etc.

- **Don't Rely on Memory Alone**

    You hear the audio once. Use the notepad effectively during the listening.

- **Time Management is Imperative**

    Don't spend too long on one question. If unsure, guess and move on.

- **Read Questions Before Listening**

    If time allows, scan the questions beforehand to know what to listen for.

- **Stay Calm and Focused**

    If you miss something, don't panic. Focus on what comes next. You may still get later answers correct!

_____

Mastering the Listening section of the CELPIP test is about more than understanding English; it's about understanding it in *context*.

In the next chapter, we will dive into the next section of the CELPIP test, which is the *Reading component*. This evaluates your ability to understand written English in everyday situations, and includes different types of reading tasks, such as reading correspondence, interpreting diagrams, and analyzing information.

Chapter 2 – Reading

"A reader lives a thousand lives before he dies ... The man who never reads lives only one."
– George R.R. Martin

Reading is powerful. It's not just about understanding the words on a page; it's about unlocking meaning, gaining insight, and discovering the world through someone else's eyes. When you read, you're not just taking in information; you are also building bridges to new ideas, cultures, and opportunities. In essence, reading helps you connect with others, solve real-life problems, and make informed decisions in your everyday life.

In the CELPIP test, the Reading section isn't just a test of your vocabulary or grammar. It's your chance to show how well you can engage with written English in real Canadian situations. This includes understanding an email from a colleague to interpreting a news article, a public notice, or even a difference of opinion in an online discussion.

In this chapter, I want to walk you through

everything you need to know, as well as what to expect, how each part of the Reading section works, and the strategies that you can use to help you stay confident and focused.

Overview

The Reading section of the CELPIP test is designed to assess your ability to read, understand, and interpret written English in a variety of everyday and workplace situations. It's not just about recognizing words or understanding grammar.

It is about making sense of real-world texts, identifying important information, and responding to what you read thoughtfully and accurately.

Throughout this section, you'll find a range of different text types, including:

- **Informal messages**, such as personal emails or notes that are normally exchanged between friends, family members, or colleagues. These texts use casual language and reflect everyday situations, so it's important to understand tone, intent, and implied meaning.

- **Formal correspondence**, including professional emails, business letters, or service-related communications. These texts are more structured and polite, and may include requests, complaints, or official information that you need to interpret and understand accurately.

- **Diagrams and charts**, where you'll be asked to apply written information to visual elements like schedules, maps, or flowcharts. These tasks test your ability to connect details between text and graphics, which is a common real-life skill in work and daily activities.

- **Factual passages**, which are often similar to short articles, company updates, or informational bulletins. These are straightforward, informative texts where understanding details, main ideas, and logical structure is crucial.

- **Opinion-based texts**, such as online discussion boards, reader forums, or blog comments, where different people express contrasting viewpoints. These passages challenge you to identify attitudes, compare perspectives, and recognize persuasive language or bias.

Each of these components is carefully designed to reflect real-life reading tasks that you might encounter living, working, or studying in an English-speaking environment — especially in Canada.

It also gives you the chance to demonstrate how

well you can interact with written English in different types of settings.

You'll be asked to do things like:

- Find the main idea of a message or article
- Understand the tone or purpose of what you're reading
- Compare different opinions
- Apply information from a text to another format, like a schedule or list

The good news is that you don't have to be an English professor or speed reader. You just need to be familiar with the tasks in this section and be able to develop smart strategies that will help you to remain calm and focused under timed conditions.

Here's what you can expect:

Section	Number of Questions
Practice Task	1
Part 1: Reading Correspondence	11
Part 2: Reading to Apply a Diagram	8
Part 3: Reading for Information	9
Part 4: Reading for Viewpoints	10

Total Time: 55 to 60 minutes

Just like the Listening section, the Reading part is broken into distinct sections that focus on real-world tasks. Each one helps you show how well you can interpret and use written information in English.

Reading Section Format & Timing

You'll be reading four different types of texts. The questions are multiple-choice, and you'll need to select the best possible answer based on what you've read.

You can go back and forth between questions during the time allowed, but it is important to remember that once time runs out, you must move to the next section.

You'll only get to complete each section once, so use your time wisely.

Scoring

Your answers are scored automatically, so the more you understand the meaning, tone, and important information in the reading passages, the higher your score. While you do not need to get every answer right for a high score, being accurate counts.

Part 1: Reading Correspondence

Here you will read an email, letter, or note. This is typically something semi-formal to informal. It could be messages between colleagues, friends, or even someone requesting services.

What You'll Be Doing:

You'll read:

- One main piece of correspondence (like an email or letter)
- Possibly a response or related follow-up
- A short set of questions. This is usually 11 in total.

What You're Being Tested On:

1. Understanding tone. Formal or Casual. (1)
2. Getting the main idea (2)
3. Identifying specific information (3)
4. Interpreting and understanding the implied meaning or attitude (4)

Sample Message (See numbers 1-4 above)

Subject: Quick Update on Friday's Team Lunch

Hi team,

Just a heads-up that our **team lunch this Friday has been moved to 1:00 PM instead of noon** (2), since the client meeting in the morning might run a bit long. **We'll still be heading to The Green Fork** (3), so no changes to the location, just the time.

Thanks to everyone who submitted their meal preferences. I've passed them along to the restaurant. And yes, they *do* have vegetarian and gluten-free options, so no need to worry! (1)

Also, just a reminder: while this lunch is a casual get-together, please remember that it's technically a **work function**, so dress appropriately and be mindful of professional behavior (especially since upper management may join us later (4)).

Looking forward to seeing you all there!

Cheers,

Maya

Strategies to Try:

1. Skim the entire message first, then go back to the questions.
2. Look for keywords in the questions and find them in the text.
3. Notice the tone. Is the writer happy? Upset? Polite? Tone can be a clue to the right answer.

If there's a follow-up reply, compare it with the original. Did anything change?

Part 2: Reading to Apply a Diagram

In this section, you will be given a diagram, like a schedule, product chart, event guide, or a how-to instruction set. You'll read a set of descriptions or short emails and then have to figure out how the diagram applies.

What You'll Be Doing:

You'll see:

- A diagram or structured graphic (like a table or schedule)
- A short-written scenario or multiple short texts
- A series of questions. This is usually 8 questions total.

What You're Being Tested On:

- Your ability to apply written information to a visual aid
- Making logical connections between texts and diagrams
- Understanding instructions, conditions, or exceptions

Scenario: Office Training Schedule

You're helping new employees at your company sign up for mandatory training sessions. Below is the weekly training schedule and a few short messages from different team members asking about availability.

Employee Training Schedule – Week of June 10th

Training Topic	Day	Time	Room	Notes
Workplace Safety	Monday	9:00–11:00 AM	201 A	All departments
Cybersecurity Basics	Tuesday	1:00–3:00 PM	104 B	IT and Admin Staff
Client Communication	Wednesday	2:00–4:00 PM	302 C	Sales & Customer Service Staff Only
Time Management	Thursday	10:00–12:00 PM	105 D	Optional – all welcome to attend
Workplace Safety	Friday	2:00–4:00 PM	201 A	Repeat session

Employee Messages

Message 1 – From Sofia (Marketing Department)

Hi! I can't make it Monday morning — is there another time I can take the Workplace Safety training?

Message 2 – From Devin (IT)

Can I attend the Time Management training? I know it's not required for my department, but I'm really interested.

Message 3 – From Priya (Customer Service)

Just confirming — my only required session is on Wednesday afternoon, right?

Message 4 – From Jonah (Admin)

Am I allowed to attend the Client Communication session too?

Sample Questions

Q1: What session can Sofia attend instead of Monday's Workplace Safety training?

Correct Answer: Friday, 2:00–4:00 PM, Room 201A

Explanation: There is a repeat of the same training on Friday at a different time — this shows the ability to apply the written request to the diagram.

Q2: Is Devin allowed to attend the Time Management training?

Correct Answer: Yes

Explanation: The notes say this session is "optional – open to all." This tests your understanding of instructions and conditions.

Q3: Which training is Priya required to attend?

Correct Answer: Client Communication on Wednesday

Explanation: She's in Customer Service, and the Client Communication training is marked as "Only for Sales & Customer Service." This tests your ability to connect a role with a restriction.

Q4: Can Jonah attend the Client Communication training?

Correct Answer: No

Explanation: Jonah is in Admin, and that session is restricted to Sales & Customer Service. These test your understanding of exceptions and limits.

Strategies to Try:

- Scan the diagram first to get a general sense of what it shows.
- For each question, go back and forth between the scenario and the diagram.
- Pay close attention to dates, times, rules, restrictions, or comparisons.
- Eliminate impossible answers. Often, two answers will be obviously wrong.

Part 3: Reading for Information

This part includes a longer, factual reading passage such as a newspaper article, report, or encyclopedia entry. It's usually written in a neutral tone.

What You'll Be Doing:

- Reading one longer passage of factual information
- Answering around 9 multiple-choice questions

What You're Being Tested On:

1. Understanding the main idea and supporting points
2. Identifying specific facts
3. Knowing the organization of the text
4. Making inferences (reading between the lines)

Example Passage – The Return of Urban Beekeeping

In recent years, cities around the world have seen a surprising trend: the rise of urban beekeeping. Once thought of as a rural-only activity, beekeeping has found a new home on rooftops, in community gardens, and even on hotel balconies in major cities like New York, Paris, and Toronto.

This movement has grown in response to increasing concerns about the decline in global bee populations. Bees are critical pollinators, responsible for the health of many plants, including fruits and vegetables. As natural habitats disappear and pesticide use increases, urban environments have become an unexpected refuge. In many cities, flowers in parks and residential gardens provide a reliable and pesticide-free source of nectar.

Urban beekeeping is not without its critics. Some experts worry about the spread of disease between densely packed hives or the potential stress on local ecosystems. Others point out that urban honeybees may compete with native pollinators for limited floral resources. However, most city beekeepers argue that the benefits — including education, local honey production, and increased pollination — outweigh the drawbacks when managed responsibly.

City governments have responded in various ways. Some have introduced licensing requirements, while others offer training programs to encourage responsible practices. Overall, urban beekeeping continues to grow as both a hobby and a community-building initiative.

Sample Questions and Explanations

Q1: What is the main idea of the passage?

A) Urban bees produce higher-quality honey than rural bees.

B) City governments are trying to eliminate urban beekeeping.

C) Urban beekeeping is increasing as a response to bee population concerns.

D) Beekeeping should only happen in rural areas.

Correct Answer: C

Explanation: The passage discusses the growth of urban beekeeping and connects it to concerns about bee population decline, which makes C the best summary.

Q2: According to the passage, why are urban environments suitable for bees?

A) Cities use more pesticides than rural areas.

B) City flowers bloom more often than rural ones.

C) Urban areas often have pesticide-free gardens.

D) Beekeeping is illegal in rural areas.

Correct Answer: C

Explanation: The passage notes that city gardens and parks often offer pesticide-free nectar, which is helpful for bees.

Q3: What is one concern raised by critics of urban beekeeping?

A) It does not produce enough honey.

B) It increases the use of pesticides.

C) It may hurt local ecosystems.

D) It makes bees less productive.

Correct Answer: C

Explanation: The text states that critics worry about stress on ecosystems and competition with native pollinators.

Q4: How is the text organized?

D) Question → Answer → Personal Opinion

C) Argument → Counterargument → Conclusion

B) Trend → Causes → Benefits & Concerns → Response

A) Problem → Solution → History

Correct Answer: B

Explanation: The passage introduces the trend, explains its causes, describes both benefits and concerns, and then mentions how governments are responding.

Q5: What can be inferred about people who support urban beekeeping?

A) They ignore the risk of disease.

B) They believe the benefits outweigh the risks.

C) They are all professional farmers.

D) They prefer city life over nature.

Correct Answer: B

Explanation: While the text mentions concerns, it also says supporters argue that benefits outweigh the drawbacks, showing belief in the value of urban beekeeping.

Strategies to Try:

1. Skim the passage once to understand the layout and topic.
2. Then tackle the questions one by one, scanning for key terms.
3. Be careful with "trap" answers! Some may sound right, but contradict the text.
4. If a question asks for the main idea, don't get distracted by details.

Part 4: Reading for Viewpoints

This part asks you to step into the shoes of different people. You'll read multiple opinions on one issue, for example, reading a collection of blog comments or forum posts.

What You'll Be Doing:

- Reading a series of short texts expressing different viewpoints
- Answering about 10 questions based on what each person says

What You're Being Tested On:

- Understanding different perspectives
- Comparing and contrasting opinions
- Picking up on attitude, tone, and intent

- Noticing bias or disagreement

Part 4 Example – Reading for Viewpoints

Scenario: Should Cities Ban Cars in Downtown Areas?

The city of Meadowville is considering a new bylaw that would ban most cars from its downtown area during peak hours, aiming to reduce traffic, cut pollution, and encourage walking and cycling. Residents were invited to share their opinions online.

Resident Comments

Comment 1 – Julia, Local Business Owner

"I understand the need to reduce emissions, but banning cars during business hours could hurt small stores like mine. Many of our customers rely on cars to pick up heavy items or visit other neighborhoods. I support environmental action, but this feels rushed and inconsiderate of local business needs."

Comment 2 – Marco, University Student

"Absolutely support the ban! The downtown core is always clogged with traffic, and it's unpleasant to walk or bike. Cities should be for people, not just vehicles. Maybe this policy will finally make Meadowville more livable and sustainable. Plus, fewer cars mean safer streets."

Comment 3 – Renée, Delivery Driver

"This will make my job harder. I already struggle to find places to park downtown. If they restrict cars, how am I supposed to deliver packages? Unless they include exceptions for service vehicles, this plan feels unfair and unrealistic."

Comment 4 – David, Retired School Principal

"I'm all for improving air quality and encouraging more walking, but I'm not sure a full ban is the answer. Why not try timed restrictions or more incentives for electric cars first? A complete ban seems extreme. Let's find a middle ground."

Sample Questions and Explanations

Q1: Whose opinion is most strongly in favor of the ban?

A) Julia

B) Marco

C) Renée

D) David

Correct Answer: B – Marco

Explanation: Marco enthusiastically supports the ban, saying cities should prioritize people over cars and praising the idea as a path to a more livable, sustainable city.

Q2: Who expresses concern about the ban's impact on daily work?

A) Julia and Marco

B) Renée and Julia

C) Marco and David

D) Renée and David

Correct Answer: B – Renée and Julia

Explanation: Renée, a delivery driver, worries about parking and logistics. Julia, a shop owner, worries about losing car-dependent customers.

Q3: Which statement best describes David's viewpoint?

A) He strongly supports the car ban with no reservations.

B) He opposes the ban entirely.

C) He prefers a more balanced or flexible approach.

D) He doesn't express an opinion.

Correct Answer: C – He prefers a more balanced or flexible approach

Explanation: David suggests alternatives like timed restrictions or incentives for electric vehicles, showing he supports the idea in principle but not in its proposed form.

Q4: What tone best describes Julia's comment?

A) Angry and dismissive

B) Neutral and factual

C) Concerned and cautious

D) Sarcastic and humorous

Correct Answer: C – Concerned and cautious

Explanation: Julia supports environmental efforts but is clearly worried about the impact on her business, expressing concern without hostility.

Q5: Which two speakers seem to disagree most strongly?

A) David and Marco

B) Julia and David

C) Marco and Renée

D) Marco and Julia

Correct Answer: D – Marco and Julia

Explanation: Marco supports the ban without hesitation, while Julia opposes it for business-related reasons. Their views contrast most directly.

Strategies to Try:

1. Always read all the viewpoints before answering.
2. Summarize each person's opinion in a word or phrase (e.g., "pro," "neutral," "against").
3. Look for strong language as it often reveals the speaker's position.
4. Be alert for subtle clues like sarcasm or qualifiers ("I guess...", "It might be...").

Reading Tips and Strategies

Even if you're a strong reader, the way you approach this test matters, especially under time pressure. The good news is that with the right habits and a little preparation, you will be able to confidently handle each question.

Here are some important reading strategies that apply to *all* parts of the CELPIP Reading section:

1. Skim, Then Dive

Before jumping into the questions, start by skimming the passage, diagram, or text provided. What's the topic? What kind of writing is it? Is it an email, a report, a casual conversation, or a forum discussion? What's the tone? Is it serious, informative, casual, or opinionated?

Skimming doesn't mean reading every single word. It means moving your eyes quickly over the text to catch the main idea, get a feel for the structure, and look for headings or keywords that might help later.

Once you've skimmed and have an idea of the layout and content, you can dive deeper into the specific parts that relate to the questions. This two-step approach saves time and helps you focus where it really matters.

2. Scan for Keywords

Instead of reading the whole passage every time you look at a new question (which takes too long and can be confusing), try to scan for keywords. That means looking for the exact words or synonyms from the question in the passage. This helps you go directly to the relevant sentence or section, rather than rereading everything.

For example, if a question asks, *"What does the writer suggest about the event's location?"*, you'd scan the passage for words like *"location," "place," "venue,"* or even phrases like *"held at"* or *"taking place in."*

Remember, you're not trying to memorize the passage; you're simply locating the part you need to answer the question accurately.

3. Eliminate Wrong Answers

Sometimes, even if you're not sure of the correct answer right away, you can improve your chances just by ruling out the ones that are clearly wrong.

Let's say you have a multiple-choice question with four options. If you can identify two that clearly don't fit (maybe they go against what the passage says, or they introduce new ideas that aren't mentioned at all), you've now got a 50/50 shot between the remaining two.

This strategy is especially helpful when you're feeling stuck. Instead of freezing or guessing blindly, shift into detective mode: look at each answer choice critically, and think, *"Does this match what I read? Or is it off?"*

This way, even if you're unsure, you're giving yourself a better chance of getting it right.

4. Don't Get Stuck on Vocabulary

It's completely normal to come across a word you've never seen before. If that happens, don't panic. Instead, look at the context. Think about what's happening in the sentence. What's the overall tone or message of the paragraph?

For example, imagine a sentence like:

"Despite the inclement weather, the outdoor ceremony went ahead as planned."

Even if you don't know the word *"inclement,"* the rest of the sentence helps you understand that the weather was probably bad, but the ceremony still happened.

5. Practice Under Timed Conditions

One of the biggest challenges on test day isn't the difficulty of the reading material; it's the clock. That's why it's so important to get comfortable with the timing of the test ahead of time.

During your practice sessions, try to simulate real test conditions. Set a timer. Limit distractions. Challenge yourself to read and answer within the same time limits you'll face during the actual exam.

Doing this helps build your test-day stamina and teaches you how to pace yourself. It also helps you get better at knowing when to move on if you're stuck, so you don't waste precious minutes on one question.

Common Challenges in the Reading Section

Even strong readers can run into challenges during the CELPIP Reading test. Test anxiety, unfamiliar wording, time pressure, or even just a moment of distraction can throw you off your game. The key is to know what might go wrong *before* test day, so you're prepared and calm if it does.

Here are some of the most common issues test-takers face, and some advice on how to handle them:

Misreading the Question

This is a surprisingly common mistake. You read the passage carefully, you know the answer — but then you misread what the *question* is actually asking. Maybe you miss a keyword like *"not"* or *"main idea"*, or you rush and assume you know what it's saying without truly processing it.

It happens! But it can cost you points.

What to do:

Slow down, just for a moment. **Take a breath.** Read the question carefully. Ask yourself:

- *What exactly is it asking me to find or understand?*
- *Are there any tricky words or negatives in the question?*
- *Is this question asking for facts, or for opinion or tone?*

Once you're clear on the question, you'll be in a much better position to choose the correct answer.

Running Out of Time

Time pressure is a real challenge in the Reading section. If you spend too long on one difficult question, you may not have enough time left to finish the rest of the section.

What to do:

Pacing is everything. Keep an eye on the clock as you move through the questions. If one question is confusing or taking too long, don't stay stuck. Flag it (if possible), make your best guess, and move on. If you have time at the end, you can come back.

The goal is to answer as many questions as possible with a calm and focused mind — not to get stuck trying to be 100% certain on one question while running out of time on five others.

Battling With a Word

Coming across a word you don't recognize can shake your confidence — but it doesn't need to. The CELPIP Reading section isn't testing your ability to define every word in the English language. It's testing your ability to understand meaning from context.

What to do:

Look at the sentence as a whole. Look at the sentences before and after it. Think about the tone of the paragraph and the situation being described.

Overthinking

We've all done it: You choose an answer, feel good about it... then you start second-guessing. *Maybe it's too obvious? What if it's a trick? Maybe that other answer is better?* And suddenly, you've talked yourself out of the right choice.

What to do:

Trust yourself. In many cases, your first instinct is the right one, especially when it's based on something you clearly saw in the text. Only change your answer if you notice something *specific* in the text that clearly supports a different choice.

Sample Questions & Answer Breakdown

Let's walk through some examples for each task type.

Example – Reading Correspondence

Email Excerpt:

Hi Jeff,

I just wanted to confirm that the Thursday meeting is now moved to Friday at 3 PM. Let me know if that works for you.

Question:

What is the main purpose of this email?

A. To cancel the meeting

B. To reschedule the meeting

C. To introduce a new project

D. To ask for Jeff's help

Correct Answer: B. The email clearly says the meeting is "moved," which means rescheduled.

Example – Reading to Apply a Diagram

Diagram:

Fitness Class Schedule:

- Monday: Yoga (10 AM)
- Tuesday: Spin (12 PM)
- Wednesday: Pilates (9 AM)

Message:

I'm free in the mornings but only before 11 AM. I'm really interested in Spin or Pilates.

Question:

Which class works best for the person?

A. Monday Yoga

B. Tuesday Spin

C. Wednesday Pilates

D. None

Correct Answer: C. Pilates is at 9 AM, and the person is available before 11 AM.

Example – Reading for Information

Passage Excerpt:

The snow leopard is one of the most elusive animals on Earth, often found in high-altitude regions.

Question:

Where are snow leopards most likely to be found?

A. Rainforests

B. Deserts

C. High-altitude regions

D. Coastal areas

Correct Answer: C. This is directly stated in the passage.

Example – Reading for Viewpoints

Viewpoints:

- **Person A:** "I think electric cars are great — they reduce emissions."
- **Person B:** "I'm not convinced. The batteries are expensive and hard to recycle."

> **Question:**
>
> Who supports electric cars?
>
> A. Both A and B
>
> B. Person A
>
> C. Person B
>
> D. Neither
>
> **Correct Answer:** B. Only Person A expresses support.

Reading is one of those skills that gets better the more you use it. Preparing for the CELPIP Reading section isn't about memorizing rules. It is about understanding ideas, tone, and intent, and reading with your brain switched on.

So read every day. Read emails, signs, news articles, and even subtitles. Practice reading in a focused, intentional way, and before you know it, this part of the CELPIP test will feel second nature.

Now that you're more confident with reading, it's time to turn your focus to the next part of the CELPIP test: the **Writing section**. This part evaluates how well you can express yourself in written English, using clear language, proper tone, and appropriate structure. You'll be asked to complete two writing tasks. One is writing an email, and the other is responding to a survey question.

Even if formal writing isn't your strength, with a little strategy and practice, you'll pass with flying colors.

Chapter 3 – Writing

"The skill of writing is to create a context in which other people can think." – **Edwin Schlossberg**

Welcome to the Writing section of the CELPIP test. In this part of the examination, you will be required to demonstrate how clearly, thoughtfully, and appropriately you can communicate in written English. The Writing component measures your ability to write for practical, everyday situations that are common in Canadian life, such as emails, surveys, and expressing opinions.

You'll be given **two tasks**, and you'll have a total of **53 to 60 minutes** to complete both.

Section	Number of Questions
Part 1: Writing an Email	1
Part 2: Responding to Survey Questions	1

Each task is designed to test different writing skills, but together, they provide a clear picture of how well you can organize your thoughts, use correct grammar and vocabulary, and adjust your tone depending on the context. The ideal word count for each task is **150 to 200 words**. It is important not just to reach the word count, but to use those words wisely.

The writing prompts are practical and realistic. For example, you might have to send a message to your landlord, respond to a neighbor's request, or give your opinion on whether the community should build a library or a gym. Your writing should be polite, logical, and organized, with appropriate vocabulary depending on whether the situation is formal or informal.

In this chapter, we'll break down both tasks, so you know exactly what to expect. You'll learn how to structure your writing, how to keep your ideas clear and connected, and how to avoid the most common mistakes. I'll also give you sample prompts, model answers, and useful phrases that will help boost your confidence.

Whether English is your first language or one you've worked hard to learn, the CELPIP Writing section gives you a chance to show your ability to express yourself clearly and effectively.

Task 1: Writing an Email

What This Task Involves

In Task 1 of the CELPIP Writing Test, you're asked to write an email based on a given situation. This task assesses your ability to communicate effectively in writing, using appropriate tone, structure, and vocabulary.

You'll be provided with a prompt that outlines a specific scenario, along with three bullet points that you must address in your email. The email should be between 150 and 200 words, and you'll have approximately 27 minutes to complete this task.

Understanding the Prompt

The prompt will present a realistic situation, such as:

- Writing to a landlord about a maintenance issue
- Contacting customer service regarding a faulty product
- Inviting a friend to an event

Each prompt will specify the purpose of the email and the points you need to cover. It's crucial to read the prompt carefully to understand the context, audience, and required tone.

Structuring Your Response

A well-structured email typically includes the following components:

- **Greeting**: Address the recipient appropriately.
  - *Formal*: "Dear Mr. Smith,"
  - *Informal*: "Hi John,"
- **Opening Statement**: State the purpose of your email clearly.
  - *Formal*: "I am writing to inform you about..."
  - *Informal*: "Just wanted to let you know..."
- **Body Paragraphs**: Address each bullet point from the prompt in separate paragraphs. Provide relevant details and maintain coherence.
- **Closing Statement**: Summarize your main points and express gratitude or anticipation.
  - *Formal*: "Thank you for your attention to this matter."
  - *Informal*: "Looking forward to hearing from you soon!"

- **Sign-off**: End with an appropriate closing phrase.
    - *Formal*: "Sincerely,"
    - *Informal*: "Best regards,"

Tone and Style: Formal vs. Informal

Determining the appropriate tone is essential. The tone should match the context and the relationship with the recipient.

- **Formal Tone**: Used when writing to someone you don't know personally, such as a company representative or official.
    - *Example*: "I am writing to express my concern regarding..."
- **Informal Tone**: Used when writing to friends, family, or colleagues.
    - *Example*: "Hey! Just wanted to check in about..."

Maintaining the appropriate tone throughout the email is crucial for clarity and professionalism.

Common Challenges

- **Maintaining Clarity**: Ensure your ideas are clearly expressed and logically organized.
- **Using the Right Tone**: Match the tone to the context and audience.

- **Addressing All Points**: Make sure to cover all bullet points provided in the prompt.

- **Staying Within Word Limit**: Aim for 150–200 words to meet the task requirements.

- **Grammar and Spelling**: Use correct grammar, punctuation, and spelling to enhance readability.

Quick Tips

- **Plan Before You Write**: Take a few minutes to outline your email, ensuring you address all required points.

- **Use Paragraphs**: Organize your email into clear paragraphs for each main idea.

- **Be Concise**: Avoid unnecessary details; focus on the main points.

- **Proofread**: Review your email for errors and clarity before submitting.

Sample Prompt and Model Answer

Prompt:

You recently subscribed to an online meal delivery service that promised healthy, gourmet meals. However, the meals delivered were not as advertised.

Write an email to the customer service department in about 150–200 words. Your email should include the following:

- Mention when and where you subscribed to the service
- Describe your dissatisfaction with the meal quality and presentation
- Request specific actions to address your disappointment

Model Answer:

Dear Customer Service Team,

I subscribed to your meal delivery service on May 1st through your website, attracted by the promise of healthy, gourmet meals.

Unfortunately, my experience has not met expectations. The meals delivered were neither fresh nor well-presented. For instance, the grilled chicken was overcooked and accompanied by soggy vegetables, which was disappointing.

I kindly request a full refund for the meals received and an explanation of how such discrepancies occurred. Additionally, I would appreciate information on steps being taken to ensure quality in the future.

Thank you for your attention to this matter. I look forward to your prompt response.

Sincerely,

[Your Name]

By understanding the structure, tone, and expectations of Task 1, and by practicing regularly, you'll enhance your ability to write effective emails in the CELPIP test. Remember to plan, write clearly, and review your work to ensure success.

Task 2: Responding to Survey Questions

In this task, you're asked to respond to a survey question that reflects everyday decisions or social issues relevant to life in Canada. This is your opportunity to share your opinion in writing clearly, confidently, and logically.

What This Task Involves

You'll be given a survey topic that asks you to choose between two options. The topics are typically drawn from everyday life, such as community decisions, workplace policies, or lifestyle preferences.

Time to complete: Around 26–27 minutes

Word count: Between **150 and 200 words**

You'll choose your preferred option and explain your reasoning using clear examples and logical arguments.

Examples of Task 2 prompts:

- Do you prefer working from home or working in the office?

- Should the community build a new park or a new library?
- Is it better for students to wear school uniforms or to dress freely?

Your job is to take a position, support it clearly, and write in a way that would make sense to a reader who knows nothing about the issue.

How to Present Your Opinion Clearly

The biggest goal in this task is to communicate your personal choice clearly and support it with convincing arguments.

Start strong with a direct opinion: "In my opinion, working from home is more beneficial than working in an office."

Then follow up with reasons and examples that connect logically to your main idea. Try to focus on two or three strong points and develop them fully.

Clarity is more important than complexity. Use straightforward language to ensure your message is easy to follow. You are not being tested on how "fancy" your vocabulary is, but on how well you communicate your ideas.

How to Organize Your Response

Great writing has a clear structure. Think of your response as a mini-essay with three main parts: an introduction, body, and conclusion.

1. Introduction (2–3 sentences)

- **State your opinion clearly**.
- Mention the two options from the prompt and declare which one you prefer.

Example:

I believe the community should build a new park instead of a library. While both options have value, I think a park would benefit more residents, especially families and children.

2. Body Paragraph(s) (6–8 sentences)

- Support your opinion with **2–3 strong points**.
- Use **specific examples** from your experience, imagination, or common situations.
- Explain **why** your choice is better than the alternative.

Example:

A park provides a place for exercise, relaxation, and social interaction. It encourages people to spend time outdoors, which is good for both mental and physical health. On weekends, families can enjoy picnics, and children have a place to play safely. This promotes a stronger sense of community.

3. Conclusion (2–3 sentences)

- Restate your main opinion in different words.
- Emphasize why your choice makes the most sense.

Example:

For these reasons, I believe a new park would serve more people in more meaningful ways than a library. It would become a space for health, connection, and joy.

Sample Prompt and Model Answer

Let's put everything together with a full sample.

Prompt:

You live in a neighborhood that is deciding how to spend funds for a community improvement project. The city council is conducting a survey.

Which do you prefer the money to be spent on?

- Building a new playground
- Improving the public library

Write 150–200 words explaining your opinion. Give reasons for your choice.

Model Answer:

I believe the money should be used to build a new playground. While improving the library has its benefits, I think a playground would be more valuable for the community as a whole.

First, a playground encourages children to be active. In today's world, many kids spend too much time indoors with screens. A safe and fun outdoor space would help promote physical activity and better health.

Second, playgrounds are great places for families to bond. Parents can spend quality time with their children, and neighbors can connect with each other. This helps build a stronger sense of community.

Lastly, libraries are still useful, but most people now access information online. A playground serves a different purpose—one that cannot be replaced digitally.

For these reasons, I strongly support building a new playground. It offers both health and social benefits that would improve the lives of many residents.

Common Challenges in Task 2

Even confident writers may face these challenges:

1. Being Too Vague

Avoid general statements like "It is good" or "It helps people." Instead, explain why or how it helps. Add specific examples.

2. Writing About Both Sides

This is not a compare-and-contrast essay. You must choose one side and support it fully. Do not say, "Both are good choices." Be decisive.

3. Repeating Ideas

Don't just repeat the same reason in different words. Make sure each paragraph adds new insight.

4. Ignoring the Word Limit

If your response is under 150 words, it may lose marks for development. If it's over 200 words, it may be penalized for lack of conciseness. Practice staying within the range.

5. Weak Conclusions

Don't just stop your writing. Wrap it up clearly by repeating your opinion and briefly reminding the reader why it matters.

Tips Specific to This Task

Here are some final tips to help you shine:

- **Choose the Side That's Easier to Support**
  - Even if it's not your real opinion, pick the option that gives you more ideas to write about.

- **Use Simple, Clear Language**
  - Avoid overly complicated words or grammar. Clear communication is key.

- **Follow a Template**
  - Using a basic structure (Intro → Body → Conclusion) can help organize your thoughts quickly under time pressure.

- **Practice Brainstorming**
  - Before you write, take 2–3 minutes to jot down your main points. This will make writing easier and faster.

- **Read Sample Answers**
  - Reading high-scoring samples can help you see what works well and how strong responses are built.

Useful Phrases and Starters

To help you get going, here are some go-to phrases you can use in your own writing:

Stating your opinion:

- I believe that...
- In my opinion...
- I strongly support...

Supporting your ideas:

- One reason is that...
- Another benefit is...
- For example...

Connecting ideas:

- In addition...
- Moreover...
- This shows that...

Concluding:

- For these reasons...
- Therefore, I believe...
- In conclusion...

Practice Exercise

Try writing your own response to the prompt below using what you've learned:

The CELPIP General Study Guide

> **Prompt:**
>
> Your local school is deciding how to improve student life. They're conducting a survey of parents and residents.
>
> Which would you prefer?
>
> - Adding more sports and outdoor activities
> - Offering more art and music classes
>
> **Instructions:**
>
> Write a 150–200-word response choosing one of the options. Explain your opinion with reasons and examples.

By understanding how to express your opinion clearly, organize your writing logically, and support your ideas with strong examples, you can feel fully prepared for Task 2 of the CELPIP Writing Test.

Achieving a high score in the CELPIP Writing section requires a blend of effective planning, strong grammar and vocabulary skills, awareness of common pitfalls, and strategic time management.

Planning Before Writing

Effective planning is the bedrock of a well-structured response. Before you begin writing, allocate 4–5 minutes to plan your response. This planning phase should include:

- **Understanding the Prompt**: Carefully read the question to grasp what is being asked.

- **Brainstorming Ideas**: Jot down key points and examples that support your response.

- **Organizing Thoughts**: Arrange your ideas logically, ensuring a clear flow from introduction to conclusion.

This approach helps in creating a cohesive and coherent response that addresses all aspects of the prompt.

Grammar and Vocabulary Expectations

Demonstrating a Strong Command of Grammar and Vocabulary

When it comes to writing, especially in a test like the CELPIP, showing that you have a strong grasp of grammar and vocabulary is absolutely essential. Your ability to express your ideas clearly and effectively depends heavily on these skills. The way you construct your sentences and the words you choose can make a huge difference in how your message is received. Let's break down the key elements you should focus on:

Varied Sentence Structures

Using a variety of sentence structures is one of the best ways to keep your writing engaging and easy to read. If every sentence is short and simple, your writing might come across as choppy or basic. On the other hand, if every sentence is long and complex, it can become confusing or tiring for the reader. The secret is balance.

Try mixing simple sentences (which have one subject and one verb) with compound sentences (which join two independent clauses with words like "and," "but," or "so") and complex sentences (which include dependent clauses). This combination not only makes your writing smoother but also demonstrates your language skills. For example:

- Simple sentence: "I enjoy reading books."
- Compound sentence: "I enjoy reading books, and I also like writing stories."
- Complex sentence: "I enjoy reading books because they help me learn new things."

Practicing this variety will improve the flow of your writing and keep your reader interested.

Appropriate Vocabulary

Choosing the right words is just as important as how you put your sentences together. Using appropriate vocabulary means selecting words that precisely convey your intended meaning. Avoid using words just because they sound "fancy" if they don't fit the context.

At the same time, don't hesitate to use more advanced words when they are appropriate—it shows your language ability. Also, steer clear of repeating the same words or phrases over and over. This can make your writing feel dull and repetitive.

Instead, try using synonyms or rephrasing ideas to add freshness to your writing. For example, instead of saying "important" multiple times, you might use "vital," "key," or "essential." This variety enriches your response and impresses examiners.

Correct Grammar Usage

Even if you have great ideas and vocabulary, poor grammar can make your response difficult to understand or appear unprofessional. Pay close attention to key grammar points such as:

- **Subject-verb agreement:** Make sure the subject and verb in each sentence agree in number (singular or plural). For example, say "She writes," not "She write."

- **Tense consistency:** Maintain the same tense throughout your response unless there is a clear reason to shift. For example, if you start describing something in the past tense, avoid switching to the present tense abruptly.

- **Punctuation:** Proper use of commas, periods, question marks, and other punctuation marks helps clarify meaning. For instance, commas can separate ideas or clauses to make sentences easier to read. Incorrect punctuation can change the meaning of a sentence or make it confusing.

Mastering these basics of grammar will ensure your writing is clear, professional, and easy for the reader to follow.

When you practice combining varied sentence structures with the right vocabulary and accurate grammar, your writing becomes polished and professional. This doesn't mean you have to write like a professor—your goal is clear, natural, and effective communication.

Practice regularly by writing different types of texts, such as emails, surveys, or short essays, and review your work for these elements. Over time, your writing will improve, and your confidence will grow.

Remember, the CELPIP Writing section isn't just about what you say; it's about how well you say it. By focusing on grammar and vocabulary, you'll create responses that are not only correct but also engaging and easy to understand. This can significantly boost your score and help you achieve the results you want.

Avoiding Common Writing Errors

Being aware of common writing mistakes is one of the best ways to improve your writing and make sure your responses stand out for the right reasons. Let's take a closer look at some of the most frequent errors that can trip up even good writers, and how to avoid them.

Repetition

One of the most common pitfalls is repeating the same words or phrases too often. When you use the same vocabulary again and again, your writing can start to sound dull and monotonous. To keep your writing fresh and engaging, try to vary your word choice.

Use synonyms or different expressions to say the same thing. For example, instead of repeatedly saying "important," you could use words like "crucial," "significant," or "essential." This not only makes your writing more interesting but also shows off your range of vocabulary, which examiners appreciate.

Spelling Mistakes

Spelling errors and typos are another common issue. Even small mistakes can distract the reader and make your writing seem careless. Plus, they can lower your overall score because they affect clarity and professionalism.

To avoid this, take time to proofread your work carefully. If you're doing the test on a computer, use any built-in spell-check tools, but don't rely on them completely—they don't catch every mistake. Developing a habit of slow, careful proofreading will help you catch those sneaky errors and polish your writing.

Lack of Clarity

Clear communication is key to good writing. Sometimes, sentences can be ambiguous or vague, leaving the reader confused about your point. This can happen if your ideas aren't fully developed, or if your sentences are too long and complicated. Aim to express one idea per sentence and use straightforward language.

If you find yourself writing something that could be interpreted in multiple ways, try to rephrase it until it's crystal clear. Using examples or explanations can also help clarify your points. Remember, clarity doesn't mean using only simple words—sometimes complex ideas need to be explained carefully, but always in a way that your reader can easily follow.

By keeping these common errors in mind and practicing strategies to avoid them, you'll make your writing stronger, easier to understand, and more enjoyable to read. And that can make all the difference when it comes to earning a high score on the CELPIP Writing section.

Time Management for Each Task

Effective time management ensures that you can plan, write, and review your responses within the allotted time. A suggested time allocation is:

- **Task 1 (Writing an Email)**:
    - Planning: 4–5 minutes
    - Writing: 18–20 minutes
    - Reviewing: 2–3 minutes
- **Task 2 (Responding to Survey Questions)**:
    - Planning: 4–5 minutes
    - Writing: 18–20 minutes
    - Reviewing: 2–3 minutes

Sticking to this schedule can help you complete each task efficiently and effectively.

Useful Phrases and Sentence Starters

Incorporating a range of phrases can enhance the quality of your writing. Here are some examples:

- **Formal Tone**:
    - *Introduction*: "I am writing to inform you about..."
    - *Requesting Action*: "I would appreciate it if you could..."
    - *Conclusion*: "Thank you for your attention to this matter."
- **Informal Tone**:
    - *Introduction*: "Just wanted to let you know..."
    - *Requesting Action*: "Could you please..."
    - *Conclusion*: "Looking forward to hearing from you soon!"
- **Expressing Opinions**:
    - "In my opinion..."
    - "I believe that..."
    - "It seems to me that..."
- **Agreeing/Disagreeing**:
    - "I completely agree with..."

- "While I understand the point, I believe..."

- **Summarizing**:
  - "In conclusion..."
  - "To summarize..."
  - "Overall, it is clear that..."

Using these phrases appropriately can make your writing more coherent and persuasive.

Understanding the Scoring Rubric

The CELPIP Writing section is evaluated based on the following criteria:

- **Content/Coherence**:
  - Relevance and clarity of ideas
  - Logical organization
  - Use of examples and supporting details

- **Vocabulary**:
  - Appropriate word choice
  - Range and precision of vocabulary

- **Readability**:
  - Sentence structure and grammar
  - Spelling and punctuation
  - Use of transitions and connectors

- **Task Fulfillment**:
  - Adherence to the task requirements
  - Appropriate tone and style
  - Completeness of the response

Understanding these criteria can help you focus on the key areas that impact your score.

Practice Example Prompts

To apply these strategies, practice with the following prompts:

Task 1: Writing an Email

Prompt: You recently purchased a product online, but it arrived damaged. Write an email to the customer service department requesting a replacement or refund.

Example Response:

Subject: Request for Replacement or Refund for Damaged Product Order #12345

Dear Customer Service Team,

I hope this message finds you well. I recently ordered a [product name] from your website (Order #12345), but unfortunately, the item arrived damaged. Upon opening the package, I noticed that the [describe damage, e.g., screen was cracked, item was broken, etc.].

I am very disappointed as I was looking forward to using this product. I would appreciate it if you could either send me a replacement or process a full refund. Please let me know what steps I need to follow to resolve this issue as soon as possible.

Thank you for your attention to this matter. I look forward to your prompt response.

Best regards,

[Your Name]

[Your Contact Information]

Task 2: Responding to Survey Questions

Prompt: Your city is considering two options for improving public transportation: expanding the subway system or adding more bus routes. Which option do you prefer and why?

Example Response:

I believe that expanding the subway system is the better option for improving public transportation in our city. While adding more bus routes might increase coverage in the short term, subways offer faster, more reliable service that can reduce traffic congestion significantly. Subways run on dedicated tracks, avoiding road traffic, which means commuters can reach their destinations more quickly during peak hours.

Moreover, subways tend to be more environmentally friendly since they produce less pollution compared to buses. Although expanding the subway requires a larger initial investment, the long-term benefits in terms of efficiency, reduced traffic, and environmental impact make it a worthwhile project. For these reasons, I support subway expansion as the preferred choice.

Now you try.

> **Practice Task 1: Writing an Email**
>
> **Prompt:**
>
> You recently stayed at a hotel during a business trip, but the room was not cleaned properly. Write an email to the hotel manager explaining the issue and requesting compensation or a solution.
>
> **Practice Task 2: Responding to Survey Questions**
>
> **Prompt:**
>
> Your community is debating whether to build a new park or a community center. Which option do you think would benefit the community more, and why?
>
> Take some time to practice writing responses to these prompts. When you do, try to focus on a

> few key things: plan out your ideas before you start writing, pay attention to your grammar and vocabulary to make sure your message is clear and polished, and keep the CELPIP scoring rubric in mind, so you know what examiners are looking for. This will help you structure your answers in a way that's organized and easy to follow.

The more you practice, the more natural writing in English will feel. You'll start to notice which phrases work best, how to connect your ideas smoothly, and how to adjust your tone depending on whether the email is formal or informal. Don't rush—take your time during practice to really think about each sentence and make sure it adds value to your response.

_____

_____

By dedicating regular practice sessions to these writing tasks and applying the strategies we've covered, you'll build confidence and improve your skills. This will definitely increase your chances of achieving a high score on the CELPIP Writing section, helping you move one step closer to your goals.

And speaking of goals, the next chapter is all about the Speaking section, where you'll get to show how well you can communicate verbally in English. We'll explore how to speak clearly and confidently, organize your thoughts on the spot, and tackle different types of speaking tasks.

Chapter 4 – Speaking

"Words are, of course, the most powerful drug used by mankind." – **Rudyard Kipling**

In this section, you will be asked to demonstrate how clearly, fluently, and confidently you can express your ideas in spoken English. The Speaking component is designed to assess your ability to communicate in real-life situations that you might encounter in everyday Canadian life. This includes things such as giving advice, describing scenes, or dealing with challenging situations.

You'll complete **eight different speaking tasks**, and the entire section will take about **15 to 20 minutes** to complete:

Section	Number of Questions
Practice Task	1
Part 1: Giving Advice	1
Part 2: Talking about a Personal Experience	1

Part 3: Describing a Scene	1
Part 4: Making Predictions	1
Part 5: Comparing and Persuading	1
Part 6: Dealing with a Difficult Situation	1
Part 7: Expressing Opinions	1
Part 8: Describing an Unusual Situation	1

Each task is designed to test different speaking skills, from how well you can tell a story or describe a picture, to how effectively you can form an opinion or respond to an unexpected scenario. When put together, these tasks provide a clear picture of your ability to speak naturally, organize your thoughts on the spot, and use the correct vocabulary and grammar.

You'll be given a short amount of time to prepare before each task (usually around 30 seconds), and then you'll be expected to speak for approximately **60 to 90 seconds**. It is important to speak clearly and naturally, with good pacing and pronunciation. Don't worry if you have an accent. What matters most is that your message is easy to understand.

The prompts are based on real-life situations, and you don't need expert knowledge either. All you need to do is practice organizing your ideas and expressing them clearly and confidently.

This section will also show you how to approach each type of question, how to structure your answers, and what the examiners are typically listening for. I'll also share helpful tips, speaking strategies, and useful phrases that will boost your fluency and help you feel more comfortable and prepared when it's time to speak.

Task 1: Giving Advice

What it involves:

You'll be presented with a situation where someone needs guidance. This could be a friend planning to make a big purchase, dealing with a challenge, or making a decision. Your task is to offer helpful and thoughtful advice.

Time: 30 seconds to prepare, 90 seconds to speak.

What examiners look for:

- Clear, organized suggestions (minimum of two).
- Empathetic and supportive tone ("I understand how you feel...")

- Use of advice phrases ("If I were you..."; "Another thing you could consider...")
- Coherent structure—introduction, advice with reasoning, conclusion.

Tips:

- Jot down two or three bullet points during prep: the problem, your advice, and a reason for each suggestion.
- Remember to use friendly, encouraging language.
- Use linking words like "firstly," "in addition," and "finally" to structure your responses.

Sample Prompt

"Your cousin wants to change careers but feels stuck and isn't sure where to start. What advice would you give them?"

Sample Response (90 seconds)

"If I were you, I'd start by thinking about what you're passionate about and what skills you already have. I think that this will help you narrow down some career ideas. Then, consider exploring online courses or certifications related to your interests. You can do these part-time while working, as it will lessen some of the pressure. Another thing to think about is

> networking: Try talking to people already working in the field you're interested in. They can probably offer you some insights, and maybe you can even find job leads. Lastly, update your resume so it shows your skills. I know it feels like it might take some time, but each move you make takes you one step closer to your dream job!"

Task 2: Talking About a Personal Experience

What it involves:

Share a real (or believable invented) personal story related to the prompt. Include details about what happened, who was involved, how you felt, and what you learned.

Time: 30 seconds to prepare, 60 seconds to speak.

What examiners look for:

- Clear narrative with a logical beginning, middle, and end.
- Accurate and consistent use of past tense.
- Relevant details and emotional engagement ("I felt...", "It was surprising...").
- Coherence and flow.

Tips:

- Select one clear and concise story.
- During prep, jot down key story elements: what, who, when, where, how you felt, and outcome.
- Focus on speaking clearly and naturally rather than overcomplicating vocabulary.

Sample Prompt

"Talk about a time when you tried a new hobby for the first time. What was it and how did it go?"

Sample Response (60 seconds)

"Last summer, I decided to try paddleboarding even though I'd never been on a board before. My friend took me to a beautiful lake near my home, and we rented boards. At first, I wobbled a lot and fell in, but I laughed every time, so it didn't frighten me. After a few tries, I found my balance and managed to paddle around the lake in peace. At the end of the day, I felt proud of myself and much more relaxed. The experience taught me that trying new things, even if they seem awkward at first, can be fun and rewarding."

Task 3: Describing a Scene

What it involves:

View an image (scene or scenario) and describe what you see. Focus on visible details—people, objects, actions, and settings.

Time: 30 seconds to prepare, 60 seconds to speak.

What examiners look for:

- Use of spatial/descriptive vocabulary ("in the foreground," "to the left," "behind").
- Clear structure: overview first, then details.
- Use of nouns and pages, verbs.
- Coherent description and logical flow.

Tips:

1. Start with a general overview ("This looks like a park in autumn.").
2. Describe from left to right or front to back.
3. Use adjectives and verbs for vividness ("two children are playing," "colorful leaves are falling").

Sample Prompt

"Here's a picture of a city square with people walking, sitting, and eating. Describe what you see."

> **Sample Response (60 seconds)**
>
> "This photo shows a busy city square on a sunny afternoon. In the foreground, a couple is sitting at a wooden table under a bright red umbrella, drinking coffee and chatting. Slightly to the left, there is a street performer playing guitar while a small group of people watches. In the background, people walk near colorful flower stands and benches. There is a young child in a blue jacket feeding pigeons by the fountain in the center. It looks like a nice place to go and meet friends, relax, and enjoy the outdoors."

Task 4: Making Predictions

What it involves:

You're given an image or scenario and asked to predict what might happen next, based on visible clues.

Time: 30 seconds to prepare, 60 seconds to speak.

What examiners look for:

- Use of future tense and modal language ("will," "might," "could").
- Logical reasoning linked to visible details.
- Multiple plausible predictions with explanations.

Tips:

- Look for visual hints like expressions, clocks, and items in motion.
- Develop 2–3 predictions logically connected to the scene.
- Use phrases such as "I think... because..." or "It's likely that..."

Sample Prompt

"You see a family struggling to push a stalled car on a dark road. What do you think will happen next?"

Sample Response (60 seconds)

"It looks like someone will call for roadside assistance soon, because fixing a car at night can be dangerous. It could also be possible that a passing driver might stop to help them. The family can also walk to the nearest service station if it is not too far away—maybe it's not too far. In any case, they'll probably resolve the situation quickly and safely, either by getting help or finding a solution together."

Task 5: Comparing and Persuading

What it involves:

You're given two options and choose one. Then you persuade the listener why your choice is better, providing reasons and addressing possible counterarguments.

Time: 60 seconds to prepare, 60 seconds to speak.

What examiners look for:

- Clear stance expressed early.
- Persuasive language ("I strongly believe," "Clearly, this option is best because…").
- At least two reasons backed by details.
- Reference or brief rebuttal of the alternative.

Tips:

- Open decisively: "I would choose option A because…"
- Give 2–3 reasons with specifics (benefits, comparisons, outcomes).
- Include a brief acknowledgment of the other option.

Sample Prompt

"Would you rather work on a team project or individually on your own? Explain why."

Sample Response (60 seconds)

"I prefer working on a team project rather than working alone. I believe that collaboration brings different ideas, and when we share perspectives, the final result is more creative and well-rounded. Second, teamwork helps with motivation and accountability, and when others rely on you, you stay focused and responsible. While working alone offers independence, it can be lonely and without much feedback. I think that teamwork not only improves the quality of work but also boosts morale and learning."

Task 6: Dealing with a Difficult Situation

What it involves:

You encounter a challenging scenario, such as handling a complaint, misunderstanding, or conflict, and you must respond appropriately, showing empathy and offering a solution.

Time: 60 seconds to prepare, 60 seconds to speak.

What examiners look for:

- Polite, empathetic tone ("I understand this is frustrating...").
- Clear problem acknowledgment.
- Specific solutions or actions.
- Professional and calm language.

Tips:

- Apologize or express empathy first.
- Outline steps to resolve.
- Use polite expressions like "I'm sorry," "Would it be helpful if..."
- Offer reassurance and a positive final statement.

Sample Prompt

"A restaurant customer complains about receiving the wrong dish and cold food. How would you handle this if you were the restaurant manager?"

Sample Response (60 seconds)

"I'm very sorry to hear about your experience. I understand how disappointing it must be to receive the wrong order and cold food. Let me fix this for you right away. I will have the right dish prepared fresh and delivered within a few minutes. In addition, I'd also like to offer this meal on the house or give you a discount on your bill as an apology. Please let me know if you'd prefer a different item or if there's anything else I can do to make your experience better."

Task 7: Expressing Opinions

What it involves:

You'll be given a general question or statement and asked to express your opinion and support it.

Time: 30 seconds to prepare, 90 seconds to speak.

What examiners look for:

- Clear statement of opinion ("In my opinion...").
- Two or three supporting reasons.
- Relevant vocabulary and examples.
- Logical structure and flow.

Tips:

- Open with your opinion clearly.
- Use linking words: "Firstly...", "Furthermore...", "Finally..."
- Support reasons with brief examples or personal insight.

Sample Prompt

"Do you think smartphones have improved our quality of life?"

> **Sample Response (90 seconds)**
>
> "In my opinion, smartphones have greatly improved our quality of life. Firstly, they keep us connected—no matter where we are, we can call or video chat with family, which strengthens relationships. Secondly, they are great tools for information—whether it's finding directions, booking appointments, or learning new skills immediately. For example, I used my phone to translate signs while traveling abroad. While excessive screen time can be a downside, the benefits, when used responsibly, far outweigh the negatives, and make life more convenient, informed, and connected."

Task 8: Describing an Unusual Situation

What it involves:

You're shown a strange or funny image and need to explain what's happening, who might be involved, and what led to it.

Time: 30 seconds to prepare, 60 seconds to speak.

What examiners look for:

- Creativity with clear structure
- Speculative language ("Maybe...", "Perhaps...")

- Descriptive language and imaginative reasoning
- Clarity in storytelling

Tips:

- Begin with a brief description of what makes the scene unusual.
- Use simple hypotheses: "Perhaps..."
- Keep your storyline logical, even if whimsical.

Sample Prompt

"Here's a picture of a dog sitting at a desk looking at a laptop. What's going on?"

Sample Response (60 seconds)

"This is a humorous picture—a dog sitting at a desk using a laptop. Perhaps it's part of a social media campaign for a pet supply store, showing how pets can 'work remotely.' Another possibility is that it's staged for a funny family photo to share with friends online. It could also be the dog's owner dressed it up for a special day at an office-themed pet event. Whatever the reason, the image is meant to be light-hearted and fun, blending everyday human behavior with the unexpected sight of a dog 'working' at a computer."

Helpful Tips

- **Note-taking matters:** Jot 3–5 bullet points during prep to stay organized.

- **Pace yourself:** Practice speaking with a timer to build comfort.

- **Use linking language:** "Firstly", "Secondly", "However", "Finally" improves clarity.

- **Record and review:** Identify areas for vocabulary, grammar, or clarity improvement.

- **Stay calm:** Use the practice task to settle nerves—examiners want natural, clear speech.

- **Be yourself:** Express your personality and reasoning—your response will be more engaging and authentic.

Mastering the CELPIP Speaking Section

1. Practice Clear & Natural Speech

- **Speak clearly, at a natural pace**—not too fast, not too slow. Pronounce each word, enunciate clearly, and pause between ideas to sound natural.

- **Volume matters**—make sure your voice isn't too quiet or too loud. Use the practice task to test your microphone and speaking style.

2. Embrace Your Accent with Confidence

- Don't obsess over your accent. Examiners care more about **clarity and accuracy** than accent.

- Use varied vocabulary and grammar to express your ideas clearly. That, above all, builds your score.

3. Use Preparation Time Wisely

- **Utilize your prep time** to organize your thoughts: Identify your main point, jot down 2–3 ideas or facts, and stick to a simple structure.

- For Tasks 5, 6, and 7 (which offer options), try practicing both choices offline.

- Once you are comfortable, **gradually reduce the preparation time** to simulate test conditions.

4. Structure Your Answers Clearly

- Start with a **direct opening**:
    - *Giving advice*: "If I were you..."
    - *Expressing opinions*: "In my opinion..."

- *Comparing and persuading*: "I strongly believe..."
- Use linking words like **"firstly," "furthermore," "however," or "finally"** to connect ideas and structure your speech.
- Conclude succinctly, reinforcing your main point: "To summarize..." or "That's why I..." effectively wraps up your response.

5. Draw from Personal Experiences

- Choose examples based on **real personal experiences** when possible—these are easier to talk about and feel more genuine.
- Even invented scenarios should reference real emotions or practicalities. It helps your response feel grounded and relatable.

6. Expand with Relevant Details

- Providing details demonstrates fluency and depth:
    - Use "because," "for example," and "such as..." to add clarity.

- Tasks 1, 2, and 6 benefit greatly from added examples and elaboration.
- Try brainstorming lots of possible details in everyday practice—this helps you think quickly during timed tasks.

7. Vary Your Vocabulary

- Avoid repeating the same words—use synonyms and paraphrasing to show your range.
- Practicing vocabulary related to common CELPIP topics (travel, education, work, community) helps you respond quickly.

8. Manage Time & Timing

- Each task has a **strict time limit**—practice with a timer to finish your thought before time runs out.
- Pause rather than rush if you're nearing the end.
- Stick to guidance:
    - Tasks 1 & 7: 30s prep + 90s speak
    - Tasks 2, 3, 4, 8: 30s prep + 60s speak
    - Tasks 5 & 6: 60s prep + 60s speak.

9. Record & Self-Evaluate

- Practice by **recording yourself**, then review: Are you clear? Fluent? Structured?
- Upgrade your responses: fix grammar, add transitions, vary your phrasing.

10. Practice Task-Specific Strategies

- Each of the eight tasks has its own strategies. General advice:
    - **Giving advice**: Show empathy, multiple solutions.
    - **Personal experience**: Be descriptive and coherent.
    - **Describing a scene**: Use spatial language.
    - **Predictions**: Use modal verbs + reasons.
    - **Comparison/persuasion**: Be firm + acknowledge the other side.
    - **Dealing with issues**: Show empathy + offer solutions.
    - **Expressing opinions**: Clear stance + supported reasons.
    - **Unusual situations**: Be creative but logical, always clear.

- These are reflected in official guides and sample responses.

11. Boost Fluency with Everyday Practice

- Incorporate **daily speaking**—in environments like home or work—to enhance natural expression.

- Use mini recording sessions—five minutes of speaking about any topic every day.

12. Be Confident, Engage the Rater

- Approach each task as a conversation—not a test. Using friendly intonation and rhythm shows whole-person proficiency.

- Imagine a real listener—this helps you speak naturally and avoid robotic tones.

13. Understand the Scoring Criteria

- Your answers are scored across four dimensions:

  - **Content/Coherence** – depth and organization of ideas

  - **Vocabulary** – range and expression

  - **Listenability** – rhythm, pauses, intonation

  - **Pronunciation** – clarity and accuracy of speech

- Aim to balance content richness with fluency and clear delivery.

14. Use Available CELPIP Resources

- Utilize **official webinars and practice materials**—these can help to familiarize you with the exam structure and expectations.

- Check out CELPIP's **YouTube "Speaking Pro" series**, which provides sample answers and expert analysis.

15. Plan a Study Routine

1. Follow the "5 minutes a day" speaking strategy: a quick prompt and timed response daily helps cement skills.
2. Weekly in-depth practice—record yourself, analyze mistakes, and review new vocabulary.

16. Focus on Strengths, Then Improve

1. Use free CELPIP practice tests and your initial recordings to identify weaknesses—whether it's vocabulary variety, structure, or speaking clarity.
2. Target your work:
   - Grammar issues? Add practice exercises.
   - Fluency gaps? Do more role-plays.

- Vocabulary limits? Brainstorm topic word lists (e.g., beach, work, family) using flashcards.

17. Final Day Reminders

1. Relax and speak naturally—your voice works better when you're calm.
2. Do a quick warm-up: speak about your day, test recording & volume.
3. Have water handy in case of a dry throat.
4. Avoid memorized responses; focus on being genuine and adaptable.

Common Mistakes in CELPIP Speaking Section

Even well-prepared test-takers can trip up during the speaking section. Two common pitfalls are issues with fluency, like pausing too much, overusing filler words, or mismanaging pacing, and content problems, such as going off-topic or giving overly short answers. Both can greatly affect your score in areas like listenability and content/coherence.

Let's talk a bit more about these common mistakes and learn how to address them effectively.

1. Pausing Too Much & Overusing Filler Words

What's happening:

You might notice yourself hesitating, adding "um," "uh," "you know," or "so" as you think through what to say. Zahn pauses become longer and more frequent, interrupting the flow of your response.

Why it matters:

Frequent hesitations and filler words can reduce your **listenability** score. Examiners rate fluency, and cluttering your speech distracts from your message and disrupts natural rhythm. According to HZad Education, these "fillers can significantly undermine your speaking marks."

How to fix it:

1. **Notice your habits** – Record yourself speaking for a minute and count your filler words.

2. **Replace fillers with pauses** – Silence is better than "um." Short pauses let you think without interruption.

3. **Practice breathing and speaking in phrases** – Plan to stop at natural sentence breaks rather than mid-thought.

4. **Do structured practice** – For each speaking task, record your response, note how many fillers appear, and practice until they drop.

2. Speaking Too Fast or Too Slow

What's happening:

In nerves, you might race through your response or drag it out, trying to fill time. Sentences become jumbled (too fast), or the response feels stilted (too slow).

Why it matters:

Pacing impacts how assessors perceive your **pronunciation** and **listenability**. Speaking too fast can make you hard to follow, while speaking too slow might indicate hesitation or lack of preparation.

How to fix it:

1. Aim for a pace similar to natural conversational English—midway between casual and super polished.

2. Practice with a timer and map your speech: 60 seconds should include an intro, development, and final summary.

3. Use breath breaks—short pauses at comma spots help maintain a steady rhythm.

3. Going Off-Topic

What's happening:

Sometimes, test-takers get excited or nervous and drift into unrelated ideas or stories.

Why it matters:

Examiners assess your ability to address the task prompt directly under **content/coherence**. If your answer diverges, you risk losing marks—regardless of how fluent or natural it sounds.

How to fix it:

1. **Identify the core question** during prep and jot it down.
2. Stick to the main prompt: "What did they ask, exactly?"
3. Avoid rabbit holes—if you start to stray, bring it back: "Going back to what you asked…"
4. In practice, pause mid-response and self-check: "Am I answering the prompt?"

4. Giving Answers That Are Too Short

What's happening:

You may deliver a concise answer, but if it doesn't meet time or word expectations, it's incomplete.

Why it matters:

Short responses can mean you've not fully developed your ideas and may be penalized in **content/coherence**.

How to fix it:

1. For 60-second tasks, offer **at least two key points with explanations**; for 90-second tasks, aim for three.

2. Use linking language to extend your response: "Firstly... secondly... finally..."

3. A quick outline helps: 10 sec stating answer + 40 sec elaboration + 10 sec closing.

5. Balancing Filler Reduction with Natural Speech

What's happening:

Overcorrection can stifle your natural flow. You might become so focused on not using fillers that your speech sounds robotic or stilted.

Why it matters:

Examiners want natural fluency as part of **listenability**. Answers should sound conversational, not choppy or memorized.

How to fix it:

1. Practice pauses fluidly—not stiff silences, but natural breaths between sentences.
2. Use conversational connectors ("however," "on the other hand," "because") instead of fillers.
3. Record yourself speaking naturally, then filter out only the problematic spots.

6. Examples to Demonstrate the Difference

Here's a before-and-after snapshot:

1. **Before** (filled with fillers and rushed):
2. "Um, I think that, uh, we should, um, build a park because, uh, it's good for, um, kids and, you know, families."
3. **After** (clear and natural):
4. "In my opinion, building a park is an excellent idea. Firstly, it gives children a safe place to play. Secondly, it allows families to spend time outdoors, which can build stronger bonds."

Notice the clarity, structure, and natural pacing.

7. Practicing Under Timed Conditions

1. Use a timer set to the task length (e.g., 60 or 90 seconds).

2. Outline your response—2–3 bullet points—for clarity.
3. Record your answer out loud as if in the test.
4. Listen back: note fillers, off-topic parts, odd pacing, or short answers.
5. Refine and re-record until your response is strong, smooth, on-topic, and filler-free.

This aligns with HZad's recommendation to practice multiple times and reduce reliance on fillers.

8. Upgrading Your Speaking with Connectors

Avoid overused conjunctions like "and," "so," or "then." Instead, elevate your language:

1. Instead of "and": use **also, furthermore, moreover**
2. Instead of "but": use **however, nevertheless, yet**
3. Instead of "so" at the end: use **therefore, overall, consequently**

This adds sophistication, boosts your **vocabulary and coherence**, and reduces filler tendencies.

9. Important Takeaways for Cleaner, Clearer Speech

Problem	How to Fix It
Filling with "um/uh"	Replace with short, confident pauses
Rushing or dragging	Time your speech; develop pacing using natural pauses
Going off-topic	Focus on prompt; self-check during response
Giving too-short answers	Bullet-point structure; develop ideas fully
Over-correcting speech	Practice balanced speech; use natural intonation

10. Tips Before Exam Day

1. **Warm up your voice**: Speak about your day casually for a minute.

2. **Set up your test space**: Check the microphone and comfort level.

3. **Breathe and relax**: A calm speaker has fewer fillers and better pacing.

4. **Ask yourself after each task:**
   - Did I address the prompt?
   - Did I speak clearly and fluently?
   - Could I reduce filler use?
   - Is my answer long enough with supporting details?

A quick mental review after each question helps maintain quality across tasks.

11. Final Encouragement

Mastering these common mistakes takes time and consistent practice, but you've already begun by being proactive. Recording yourself, analyzing your speech, and focusing on clarity, structure, and natural rhythm will dramatically improve your speaking performance. Remember:

1. **Less filler** = higher fluency score
2. **Steady pace** = better pronunciation and comfort
3. **On-topic, well-developed answers** = stronger content marks
4. **Natural language and connectors** = superior coherence and vocabulary

If you apply these strategies daily, and especially in practice timed conditions, you'll develop the speaking habits that examiners value most.

Useful Phrases & Expressions

1. Conversational Vocabulary (Everyday Speech)

Choosing vocabulary that feels natural and conversational helps your score—overly formal words can sound out of place in speech.

Word/Phrase	Meaning	Example
cozy	*comfortable and warm*	"The cafe was cozy, with soft lights and comfy chairs."
rigorous	*thorough and detailed*	"We did a rigorous training program before starting."
rehearse	*practice*	"I rehearse my speech until it flows smoothly."
enthusiasm	*eagerness*	"Her enthusiasm for the project was contagious."
fond	*having a liking for something*	"I'm fond of long summer evenings by the lake."

urge	*strongly encourage*	"I urge you to try volunteering—it's rewarding."
tremble	*shake slightly*	"My hands would tremble before I spoke on stage."
plethora	*a large amount*	"There's a plethora of online courses to choose from."

Tip: Start with everyday words and phrases, then sprinkle in expressive adjectives or collocations for richness—and stay away from stuffy or formal language.

2. Sentence Starters & Transitions

Smooth transitions and clear openings help your speech flow naturally. CELPIP's own study pack recommends:

1. **Giving Advice:** "If I were you, I'd...", "Another thing you could do is...", "One final thing is..."

2. **Expressing opinions:** "In my opinion...", "I strongly believe that...", "From my perspective..."

3. **For descriptions:** "In the foreground...", "To the left...", "Behind that..."

Using these phrases establishes structure and guides the listener clearly through your thoughts.

3. Connecting Ideas Clearly

To ensure your responses are structured and smooth:

1. **First/Firstly**
2. **Secondly/Next**
3. **Moreover/Furthermore**
4. **However/On the other hand**
5. **Finally/Lastly**
6. **In conclusion/To summarize**

Example:

"Firstly, I believe... Secondly, another benefit is... Furthermore, it's more convenient... Finally, that's why I prefer..."

These connectors are simple but powerful—they show coherent thinking and logical flow.

4. Expressions for Giving Advice

When someone needs guidance, use:

1. "If I were you, I would..."
2. "Another thing you might consider is..."
3. "It may help to..."
4. "One final suggestion is..."

Supported by reasons:

"If I were you, I would look at online reviews—researching a product thoroughly helps avoid surprises."

5. Useful Phrases for Sharing Opinions

Sound confident and clear:

1. "In my opinion... / I believe that..."
2. "I strongly think..."
3. "From my perspective..."
4. "It seems to me that..."
5. "Personally, I feel..."
6. "I'm convinced that..."

Add reasons:

"In my opinion, working remotely boosts productivity for two reasons..."

6. Speculating & Predicting

When predicting from a photo or scenario:

1. "It looks like..."
2. "Perhaps..."
3. "I imagine that..."
4. "I think it might..."
5. "It's likely that..."

Examples:

"It looks like they're waiting for a bus, so perhaps the bus will arrive soon."

"I imagine this won't last long, because the weather station predicts rain."

7. Idioms & Collocations

Idiomatic language adds natural flow. Use carefully:

1. **Memories came flooding back** – recalling events

"When I revisited my old school, memories came flooding back."

1. **Bring back memories** – evoke remembrance

"Talking about childhood trips always brings back memories."

1. **Safe bet** – reliable choice

"Choosing public transport is a safe bet if you want to avoid parking fees."

1. **Worthwhile** – valuable or beneficial

"Volunteering at the shelter was worthwhile—it felt good to help."

Collocations are also key; combining words naturally ("have a relaxing weekend," "strongly believe," "deep concern") enhances fluidity

8. Expressions for Offering Help or Empathy

In Task 6 (dealing with a situation), you might use:

1. "I'm sorry to hear that..."
2. "I understand how frustrating that must be..."
3. "Let me see what I can do to help."
4. "Would it help if I...?"
5. "I'll make sure this gets resolved."

These convey care and professionalism.

9. Closing or Summarizing Phrases

End your answers clearly.

1. "In conclusion, ..."
2. "To sum up, ..."
3. "Overall, I think..."
4. "That's why I believe..."

These signal the end, helping you wrap up neatly within time limits.

> **Sample Response Incorporating Phrases**
>
> Prompt: *"Would you prefer working from home or in an office? Explain why."*
>
> **Response (90 sec):**
>
> "In my opinion, working from home is a better option for many people. Firstly, it reduces commute time, which means more free time for personal pursuits. For example, instead of sitting in traffic, I can use that hour to exercise or prepare a healthy breakfast. Secondly, a home environment can be quieter and more focused, allowing for greater productivity. However, I understand that it may feel isolating for some, so it's important to schedule virtual check-ins with colleagues. Overall, the flexibility and efficiency of remote work make it a more appealing choice for me."
>
> *Key phrases used:*
>
> 1. "In my opinion..."
> 2. "Firstly... Secondly..."
> 3. "For example..."
> 4. "However, I understand that..."
> 5. "Overall..."

10. Practice Tips

1. **Learn a few phrases for each task type.** Make flashcards or a phrase list.

2. **Use role-play or self-recording.** Try to integrate multiple phrases naturally.

3. **Focus on fluency, not perfection.** Sounding over-rehearsed can harm "listenability."

4. **Balance complexity and comfort.** Use expressive phrases within your speaking range.

11. Summary of Key Phrases

Task	Phrases
Giving Advice	"If I were you...", "Another thing you could do is...", "One final suggestion is..."
Expressing Opinions	"In my opinion...", "I strongly believe...", "From my perspective..."
Describing A Scene	"In the foreground...", "To the left...", "Behind that..."
Predicting	"It looks like...", "Perhaps...", "I imagine that..."

Speculation	"Maybe...", "It's likely that..."
Helping/Empathy	"I understand how you feel...", "Would it help if...?"
Closing	"Finally...", "In conclusion...", "To summarize..."
Connectors	"Firstly, Secondly, Lastly", "However", "Moreover", "Because"

By using these useful phrases and expressions in your preparation, you'll improve the structure, coherence, and natural flow of your speaking responses. Try to learn them in clusters, practice in context, and use them confidently on test day.

Mini Speaking Practice Test

This section gives you a realistic feel for what to expect in the speaking component of the CELPIP test. There are eight tasks, each focusing on a different real-life communication skill. You'll get a sample prompt, clear task instructions, timing details, and a sample response for each one.

Remember: each task is time-limited and designed to simulate practical, everyday situations in Canada. Practice speaking clearly, with confidence, and stay focused on your message.

General Tips Before You Start

1. You get **30 seconds to prepare** for each task (except Task 3).

2. Your **response time** is **60 to 90 seconds**, depending on the task.

3. Use natural, everyday vocabulary. Speak clearly and at a steady pace.

4. Structure your responses: introduction, supporting points, and a conclusion.

5. Avoid long pauses or filler words like "um," "you know," or "like."

Task 1: Giving Advice

What you're asked to do: Give advice to a friend who needs help making a decision.

Prep Time: 30 seconds

Response Time: 90 seconds

Sample Prompt: Your friend just got a job offer in another city. They're unsure whether to move. Give your advice.

How to Approach:

Start by acknowledging their situation, then give 2–3 strong points in support of your advice. Finish with encouragement.

Sample Response:

"Hi! Congratulations on the job offer—that's exciting! If I were you, I'd seriously consider moving. First, it's a great opportunity to grow your career and gain new experiences. Also, living in a new city can be a refreshing change. You'll meet new people and explore new places. Of course, it's tough to leave your comfort zone, but I think the benefits outweigh the risks. If it doesn't work out, you can always come back, but at least you'll know you tried. I say go for it!"

Task 2: Talking About a Personal Experience

What you're asked to do: Describe something from your own life—a memory or an event.

Prep Time: 30 seconds

Response Time: 60 seconds

Sample Prompt: Talk about a time you helped someone.

How to Approach:

Use the past tense, describe the situation clearly, and end with what you learned or how it made you feel.

Sample Response:

"One time, I helped my neighbor carry her groceries up the stairs. She's an elderly lady, and it was snowing outside, so the steps were slippery. I saw her struggling and offered to help. She was so thankful and gave me a big smile. It only took a minute of my time, but it made her day, and mine, too. It reminded me how small acts of kindness can make a big difference."

Task 3: Describing a Scene

What you're asked to do: Describe what's happening in a photo.

Prep Time: 0 seconds (starts immediately!)

Response Time: 60 seconds

Sample Prompt: [Imagine a photo of a busy park on a sunny day.]

How to Approach:

Focus on the foreground, middle, and background. Describe people, actions, and emotions.

Sample Response:

"In the foreground, there's a family sitting on a picnic blanket. The parents are eating, and their kids are playing with a ball. In the middle of the park, a man is jogging, and there's a couple walking their dog. In the background, I see trees, and a group of teenagers is playing guitar and singing. Everyone looks happy and relaxed. It looks like a lovely day to be outside."

Task 4: Making Predictions

What you're asked to do: Look at a situation and predict what might happen next.

Prep Time: 30 seconds

Response Time: 60 seconds

Sample Prompt: You see a child trying to reach a shelf in a grocery store.

How to Approach:

Use future tense and phrases like "I think," "maybe," "it looks like," or "it's likely that..."

Sample Response:

"It looks like the child is trying to reach something, but the shelf is too high. I think he might call his parent or ask someone nearby for help. Maybe a store employee will notice and give him a hand. If he tries to climb, it could be dangerous, so I hope someone helps him soon."

Task 5: Comparing and Persuading

What you're asked to do: Choose between two options and convince someone that your choice is better.

Prep Time: 30 seconds

Response Time: 60 seconds

Sample Prompt: Your community is planning to build either a swimming pool or a gym. Choose one and explain why.

How to Approach:

Choose clearly, give at least two reasons, and sound enthusiastic.

Sample Response:

"I think a swimming pool would be a better choice for our community. First, swimming is a great full-body workout for people of all ages, including seniors and children. Second, it's more fun and relaxing, so families can enjoy it together. While gyms are great, we already have a few nearby, but there's no public pool. A swimming pool would benefit more people."

Task 6: Dealing with a Difficult Situation

What you're asked to do: Respond to a stressful or awkward situation calmly and helpfully.

Prep Time: 30 seconds

Response Time: 60 seconds

Sample Prompt: You booked a hotel room, but it wasn't clean. Speak to the manager.

How to Approach:

Stay polite and explain the problem clearly. Ask for a reasonable solution.

Sample Response:

"Hi, I just checked into room 204, and I noticed that the bathroom wasn't cleaned properly. There were towels on the floor, and the bin was full. I'd appreciate it if someone could come and take care of it. I understand these things happen, but I hope it can be fixed soon. Thank you for your help."

Task 7: Expressing Opinions

What you're asked to do: Share your opinion on a topic and support it with reasons.

Prep Time: 30 seconds

Response Time: 90 seconds

Sample Prompt: Do you think students should wear uniforms in school?

How to Approach:

State your opinion clearly, give 2–3 reasons, and conclude.

Sample Response:

"In my opinion, students should wear uniforms. First, it promotes equality, and everyone looks the same, so there's less pressure to wear expensive clothes. Second, it helps students focus on learning instead of fashion. Uniforms also create a sense of discipline and school pride. While some argue it limits expression, students can still express themselves in other ways. Overall, uniforms have more benefits."

Task 8: Describing an Unusual Situation

What you're asked to do: Describe something surprising, strange, or unexpected to someone.

Prep Time: 30 seconds

Response Time: 60 seconds

Sample Prompt: You saw someone walking a goat in the city. Call your friend and describe it.

How to Approach:

Be vivid and excited. Use humor or surprise naturally.

Sample Response:

"Hey, you won't believe what I just saw. I was walking downtown, and this guy was walking a goat on a leash! People were stopping to take pictures, and the goat seemed totally calm, just

> trotting along like a dog. It even had a little jacket on! I've never seen anything like that before. It made my whole day."
>
> Practice each of these speaking tasks often. The more you prepare, the more confident and fluent you'll become. Make sure you're not just speaking, but speaking with structure, clarity, and purpose. Use a timer, record yourself, and review your recordings to improve.

This chapter has provided you with a solid foundation and clear understanding of the CELPIP – General Test—its purpose, format, and what skills it evaluates. With this background, you're now better prepared to move forward with confidence.

The next step is all about practice. In the upcoming chapter, we will explore sample questions and answers that closely resemble those found on the actual CELPIP – General Test. This will help you apply what you've learned, develop effective strategies, and build the confidence needed to perform well on test day. Be sure to review them carefully to ensure you're fully prepared and confident when test day arrives. Get ready to put your preparation into action.

Chapter 5 – Practice Test Questions & Answers

"Practice isn't the thing you do once you're good. It's the thing you do that makes you good."— **Malcolm Gladwell**

This section contains **two full-length CELPIP General Practice Tests**, each designed to closely mirror the official test format. You'll find all four skill areas—Listening, Reading, Writing, and Speaking—along with detailed instructions, realistic questions, and answer keys. Use these mock tests to assess your current level, identify areas for improvement, and build confidence. After completing each test, review the included **model answers and scoring guides** to better understand what's expected and how to boost your performance on test day.

Before we begin the test, here is a full breakdown of the test format:

The CELPIP General Study Guide

CELPIP General Test Format

1. Listening (47–55 minutes)

Number of Parts: 6

Question Types:

Part	Task Description	No of Questions
1	Listening to Problem Solving	8
2	Listening to a Daily Life Conversation	5
3	Listening for Information	6
4	Listening to a News Item	5
5	Listening to a Discussion	8
6	Listening to Viewpoints	6

Audio is played **once only**.

2. Reading (55–60 minutes)
Number of Parts: 4
Question Types:

Part	Task Description	No of Questions
1	Reading Correspondence	11
2	Reading to Apply a Diagram	8
3	Reading for Information	9
4	Reading for Viewpoints	10

Read emails, advertisements, opinion pieces, articles, etc.

3. Writing (53–60 minutes)
Number of Tasks: 2
Question Types:

Task	Task Description	Word Count
1	Writing an Email	150–200
2	Responding to Survey Questions	150–200

You'll write an email responding to a situation (e.g., complaint, request). You'll express and justify opinions in the survey response task.

4. Speaking (15–20 minutes)
Number of Tasks: 8
Question Types:

Task	Task Description	Time Given
1	Giving Advice	90 seconds
2	Talking about a Personal Experience	90 seconds
3	Describing a Scene	90 seconds
4	Making Predictions	90 seconds
5	Comparing and Persuading	60 sec prep + 90 sec response
6	Dealing with a Difficult Situation	60 sec prep + 90 sec response
7	Expressing Opinions	60 sec prep + 90 sec response
8	Describing an Unusual Situation	60 sec prep + 90 sec response

You speak into a microphone; responses are recorded and assessed by CELPIP raters. Tasks mimic real-life situations in Canada.

Fred Winstone

CELPIP Mock Test 1 – Full Questions

LISTENING SECTION

Time: 46–55 minutes

Parts: 6

Total Questions: 38

Remember that the videos can only be played once during the actual examination.

Part 1: Listening to Problem Solving (8 Questions)

> **Video Transcript:** (Two friends, Jason and Mia, are discussing weekend plans.)
>
> **Jason:** Hey Mia, have you made any plans for this weekend? I was thinking of doing something fun like hiking outdoors.
>
> **Mia:** Actually, I was just going to stay in and catch up on my reading. But I could be convinced to join you. What do you have in mind?
>
> **Jason:** Well, I was thinking either a hike up Bluebird Trail or maybe kayaking on Lake Pineview. The weather's supposed to be nice.
>
> **Mia:** Hmm, both sound great. But didn't you say your kayak had a leak?

> **Jason:** Yeah, but I got it patched last weekend. It's good to go!
>
> **Mia:** Okay, in that case, kayaking sounds like a lot of fun. Do we need to bring anything?
>
> **Jason:** Just sunscreen, water bottles, and maybe a snack or two. I'll bring the life jackets.
>
> **Mia:** Perfect. Saturday morning?
>
> **Jason:** Yep. I'll pick you up at 9.

Questions:

1. What activity does Jason suggest first?

    A. Reading

    B. Hiking

    C. Fishing

    D. Watching a movie

2. What was Mia originally planning to do?

    A. Go shopping

    B. Visit a friend

    C. Stay in and read

    D. Go hiking

3. Why was Mia hesitant about kayaking?

    A. She can't swim

    B. Jason's kayak had a leak

C. She didn't have a life jacket

D. The weather was bad

4. What did Jason do to his kayak recently?

    A. Sold it

    B. Bought a new one

    C. Patched a leak

    D. Painted it

5. What does Mia need to bring?

    A. Kayak and paddle

    B. Life jacket

    C. Sunscreen and snacks

    D. Tent and sleeping bag

6. What time will Jason pick Mia up?

    A. 8 am

    B. 9 am

    C. 10 am

    D. 11 am

7. What day are they planning their outing?

    A. Friday

    B. Saturday

    C. Sunday

    D. Monday

8. What is the weather expected to be like?

   A. Rainy

   B. Cloudy

   C. Nice

   D. Cold

Part 2: Listening to a Daily Life Coversation (5 Questions)

> **Video Transcript:** (Two coworkers, Priya and Daniel, chatting at the office)
>
> **Priya:** Daniel, have you seen the coffee machine this morning?
>
> **Daniel:** Yeah, it's not working again. I tried turning it off and on, but no luck.
>
> **Priya:** That's the third time this week. I really think we need a new one.
>
> **Daniel:** Totally agree. I was thinking of sending a note to the office manager.
>
> **Priya:** Do it! And maybe suggest a model that has a built-in grinder.
>
> **Daniel:** Good idea. I'll check a few options online during my lunch break.
>
> **Priya:** Thanks! In the meantime, I guess it's back to instant coffee.

Questions:

1. What is the main problem discussed?

   A. The printer is jammed

   B. The coffee machine is broken

   C. There are no cups

   D. The microwave isn't working

2. How many times has this issue occurred this week?

   A. Once

   B. Twice

   C. Three times

   D. Four times

3. What does Priya suggest?

   A. Buying more coffee

   B. Cleaning the machine

   C. Replacing the coffee machine

   D. Making tea instead

4. What type of coffee machine does Priya prefer?

   A. One that makes espresso only

   B. One with a grinder

   C. One with a timer

   D. One that uses pods

5. What will Daniel do next?

    A. Call a repairman

    B. Write to the office manager

    C. Make coffee himself

    D. Go out to buy coffee

Part 3: Listening for Information (6 Questions)

> **Video Transcript:** (A radio panel discussion)
>
> **Moderator:** Welcome back to "Community Perspectives." Today we're discussing remote work. With me are Sarah, a tech consultant, and Kevin, a small business owner. Sarah, let's start with you.
>
> **Sarah:** Thanks. I think remote work has proven it can be just as effective as in-office work. It gives employees flexibility, and for many, it improves mental health.
>
> **Kevin:** That's true for some industries, but in my experience, running a café, remote work just isn't practical. I need my staff physically present.
>
> **Sarah:** Sure, that makes sense for service jobs. But even in other sectors, I've seen employers resist remote work unnecessarily.

Kevin: But don't you think people can get isolated? My niece started working from home and said she felt really disconnected after a while.

Sarah: That's a fair point. It does depend on personality. I just think businesses should trust their teams more.

Moderator: Great points. It seems there's no one-size-fits-all.

Questions:

1. What is the main topic of discussion?

    A. Workplace safety

    B. Employee training

    C. Remote work

    D. Job interviews

2. What is Sarah's job?

    A. Café manager

    B. Journalist

    C. Tech consultant

    D. Lawyer

3. What benefit of remote work does Sarah mention?

   A. Increased salary

   B. Better mental health

   C. Easier hiring

   D. Free equipment

4. Why does Kevin disagree with Sarah?

   A. He dislikes technology

   B. He can't afford remote tools

   C. His business requires physical presence

   D. He believes in strict rules

5. What does Kevin say about his niece?

   A. She got promoted

   B. She started working at a café

   C. She felt isolated from working at home

   D. She quit her remote job

6. What is Sarah's suggestion to businesses?

   A. Pay more bonuses

   B. Limit working hours

   C. Trust their employees

   D. Buy better software

Part 4: Listening to a News Item (5 Questions)

> **Video Transcript:** (A radio news report)
>
> **News Anchor:** In local news today, a new pedestrian bridge has opened over Highway 16, linking the east and west sides of Riverview Park. The bridge was completed two months ahead of schedule and under budget, costing $3.2 million. City councilor Janet Lee praised the project as an example of efficient planning and community consultation.
>
> The bridge is part of a larger revitalization effort aimed at making the park more accessible and encouraging active transportation. Already, residents are taking advantage of the crossing. Local runner Ben Carter says it's now easier to get to his favorite jogging trail without worrying about traffic.

Questions:

1. What is the news item about?

    A. A new subway line

    B. A newly constructed pedestrian bridge

    C. A school renovation project

    D. A road closure

2. Where is the bridge located?

   A. Over a river

   B. Through downtown

   C. Over Highway 16

   D. Inside a sports complex

3. How was the project described by Janet Lee?

   A. Too expensive

   B. Poorly planned

   C. An example of community collaboration

   D. A short-term fix

4. What is the purpose of the bridge?

   A. To reduce traffic congestion

   B. To connect businesses

   C. To improve access to a park

   D. To reach a shopping mall

5. Who is Ben Carter?

   A. The mayor

   B. A city planner

   C. A local runner

   D. A construction worker

Part 5: Listening to a Discussion (8 Questions)

> **Video Transcript:** (University students Maya and Leo talking about a group project)
>
> **Maya:** Leo, we really need to divide the work for this history project. It's due next Friday.
>
> **Leo:** I agree. I can handle the research on World War I battles if you want to take the political causes.
>
> **Maya:** Sure. I'll also start putting the slides together. Are you okay writing the conclusion?
>
> **Leo:** Yeah, no problem. I'll try to have everything ready by Wednesday so we can review it together.
>
> **Maya:** That's perfect. Let's meet on campus Thursday morning to rehearse.
>
> **Leo:** Sounds good. I'll book a study room in the library.

Questions:

1. What is the topic of the students' project?

    A. Political science

    B. Ancient history

    C. World War I

    D. Modern economics

2. When is the project due?

   A. Wednesday

   B. Thursday

   C. Friday

   D. Monday

3. What section will Maya work on?

   A. Battles only

   B. Political causes and slides

   C. Timeline and bibliography

   D. Only the conclusion

4. When will they meet to rehearse?

   A. Wednesday afternoon

   B. Thursday morning

   C. Friday at noon

   D. Tuesday after class

5. Where will they meet?

   A. Maya's house

   B. Their classroom

   C. At a coffee shop

   D. In the library

6. **Who will write the conclusion of the project?**

7. A. Maya

8. B. Leo

9. C. Both of them together

10. D. They haven't decided yet

11. **What does Leo agree to do first?**

12. A. Create the slides

13. B. Book a study room

14. C. Research World War I battles

15. D. Edit Maya's section

16. **What is their plan for Wednesday?**

17. A. Meet on campus to rehearse

18. B. Submit the project

19. C. Finalize the slides together

20. D. Have Leo's part ready to review

Part 6: Listening to Viewpoints (6 Questions)

> **Video Transcript:** (Is It Okay to Outgrow Old Friendships?)
>
> **Speaker 1 – Alia:**
>
> I used to feel really guilty about drifting apart

from some of my old friends. But now I realize it's just part of growing up. We change. Our values shift. I'm still grateful for those memories, but I don't want to force connections that no longer feel real. Life's too short for one-sided friendships. I'd rather focus on relationships that feel mutual, supportive, and honest.

Speaker 2 – Jacob:

I hear that, but I also think we give up on people too easily these days. Friendships go through rough patches just like any relationship. Maybe your friend is going through something, and pulling away doesn't mean they've stopped caring. Sometimes we just need to show up, even when it's uncomfortable. Long friendships are rare, and I think they're worth holding onto if we can.

Questions

1. What are Alia and Jacob mainly talking about?
2. A. How to make new friends as an adult
3. B. Whether it's okay to let go of old friendships
4. C. The best ways to deal with loneliness
5. D. How to host better social events

6. Why does Alia believe it's okay to let go of some friendships?
7. A. She prefers to be alone
8. B. She doesn't value long-term relationships
9. C. She believes friendships should feel mutual and real
10. D. She moved to a different city
11. What is Jacob's main concern about ending friendships?
12. A. That people don't take relationships seriously anymore
13. B. That people don't have time for socializing
14. C. That it's impossible to make new friends
15. D. That old friends can become enemies
16. What does Alia say about her past friendships?
17. A. She regrets them deeply
18. B. She wants to rekindle them
19. C. She appreciates them but doesn't want to force anything
20. D. She thinks they were a waste of time

21. What does Jacob suggest about friendships?

22. A. They should always feel easy

23. B. It's best to replace them often

24. C. They are only valuable if they benefit you

25. D. They sometimes require showing up even when it's hard

26. How do Alia and Jacob's views differ?

27. A. Alia prefers to hold on; Jacob prefers to let go

28. B. Alia sees change as natural; Jacob values trying to maintain long-term connections

29. C. Alia believes all friendships are forever; Jacob thinks they're temporary

30. D. Alia wants more friends; Jacob wants fewer

> **READING SECTION**
>
> **Time:** 43–56 minutes
>
> **Parts:** 4
>
> **Total Questions:** 38

Part 1: Reading Correspondence (11 Questions)

Read the email below and answer questions 1-10.

Subject: Invitation to Company Workshop

Dear Team,

We are excited to announce a workshop on "Effective Communication" scheduled for next Friday, October 20th, from 9 am to 4 pm in Conference Room B. This session will help improve your presentation skills and teamwork.

Please confirm your attendance by October 15th. Lunch and refreshments will be provided. If you have any questions, feel free to contact HR.

Best regards,

Melissa Memel

HR Manager

1. What is the main purpose of this email?

A) To invite staff to a workshop.

B) To announce a new company policy.

C) To request feedback from employees.

D) To schedule performance reviews.

2. When will the workshop take place?

A) October 15th.

B) October 20th.

C) October 21st.

D) October 25th.

3. What is the topic of the workshop?

A) Time management.

B) Stress relief.

C) Effective communication.

D) Customer service.

4. Where will the workshop be held?

A) Main office lobby.

B) Conference Room A.

C) Conference Room B.

D) Offsite location.

5. What should employees do if they want to attend?

A) Show up on the day.

B) Confirm attendance by October 15th.

C) Contact the trainer directly.

D) Pay a fee to participate.

6. What will be provided during the workshop?

A) Training materials only.

B) Lunch and refreshments.

C) Certificates of completion.

D) Free transportation.

7. Who sent the email?

A) Workshop trainer.

B) HR Manager.

C) Company CEO.

D) Team leader.

8. How should employees respond if they have questions?

A) Email their supervisor.

B) Contact HR.

C) Attend the workshop and ask in person.

D) Call the trainer's phone number.

9. What is NOT mentioned about the workshop?

A) Its duration.

B) The specific location.

C) The cost.

D) The names of participants.

10. Why might the company offer this workshop?

A) To increase productivity.

B) To improve employee satisfaction.

C) To reduce workplace conflicts.

D) Presentation skills and teamwork.

11. What tone does the email use?

A) Formal and enthusiastic

B) Informal and casual

C) Strict and demanding

D) Humorous and lighthearted

Part 2: Reading to Apply a Diagram (8 Questions)

Refer to the floor plan below of a library and answer questions 1-8.

[Look at the simple floor plan of a library with areas marked: Entrance, Circulation Desk, Reading Area, Computer Stations, Children's Section, Study Rooms, Restrooms, Café.]

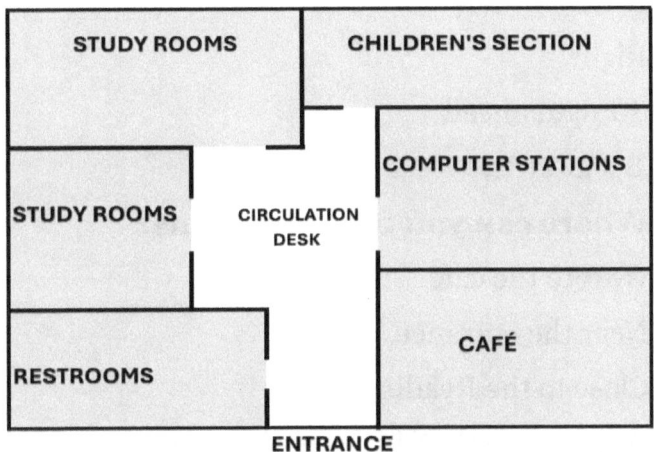

1. Where is the Circulation Desk located?

A) Near the entrance.

B) Next to the café.

C) In the Children's Section.

D) In between the study rooms and computer stations.

2. Which area is closest to the Computer Stations?

A) Study Rooms.

B) Children's Section.

C) Reading Area.

D) Circulation Desk

3. If you enter the library, which direction should you go to reach the Study Rooms?

A) Left.

B) Right.

C) Straight ahead.

D) Backwards.

4. Where can you find restrooms?

A) Next to the café.

B) Near the entrance.

C) Close to the Reading Area.

D) Adjacent to the Children's Section.

5. Which section is designed for younger visitors?

A) Children's Section.

B) Reading Area.

C) Study Rooms.

D) Computer Stations.

6. If someone wants to buy a coffee, where should they go?

A) Near the entrance.

B) Next to the restrooms.

C) Café.

D) Circulation Desk.

7. What is the purpose of the Circulation Desk?

A) To borrow and return books.

B) To read newspapers.

C) To access computers.

D) To buy snacks.

8. Which area is likely the quietest?

A) Café.

B) Children's Section.

C) Study Rooms.

D) Entrance.

Part 3: Reading for Information (9 Questions)

Read the following article and answer questions 1-10.

Title: The Benefits of Urban Gardening

Urban gardening is becoming extremely popular. That's because more and more people want to grow their own food and feel connected to nature, even in the middle of the city. Urban gardening involves growing plants, vegetables, and herbs in small spaces such as balconies, rooftops, or even community gardens.

There are a lot of advantages to urban gardening. First, it promotes healthier eating by providing fresh, organic produce. Second, it helps reduce the carbon footprint as it lowers the need to transport food over long distances. Third, gardening is a great stress reliever and is also a wonderful way to be physically active.

Moreover, urban gardens play a role in improving local biodiversity by attracting pollinators, such as bees and butterflies. They also help cool down cities by giving shade and reducing heat absorption from concrete.

Despite its many benefits, urban gardening can be challenging due to limited space, soil contamination, and access to water. However, with proper planning and some community support, these obstacles can be overcome.

1. What is urban gardening?

A) Farming in rural areas.

B) Growing plants in small city spaces.

C) Planting trees in parks.

D) Using greenhouses for crops.

2. Why is urban gardening beneficial for health?

A) It increases exercise only.

B) It provides fresh, organic food.

C) It reduces pollution completely.

D) It decreases food costs drastically.

3. How does urban gardening help the environment?

A) By increasing transportation needs.

B) By reducing food transport distances.

C) By removing pollinators.

D) By increasing concrete areas.

4. What is one mental benefit of gardening mentioned?

A) Increases stress levels.

B) Causes boredom.

C) Relieves stress.

D) Limits social interaction.

5. What animals are attracted to urban gardens?

A) Birds and squirrels.

B) Bees and butterflies.

C) Cats and dogs.

D) Fish and frogs.

6. How do urban gardens affect city temperatures?

A) They increase heat absorption.

B) They provide shade and cool down cities.

C) They have no effect.

D) They increase pollution.

7. What is a common challenge for urban gardening?

A) Too much space.

B) Soil contamination.

C) Lack of interest.

D) Excess water availability.

8. How can challenges in urban gardening be solved?

A) Ignoring problems.

B) With planning and community support.

C) By using pesticides heavily.

D) By avoiding gardening altogether.

9. What spaces are used for urban gardening?

A) Large farms only.

B) Balconies, rooftops, and community gardens.

C) Forests.

D) Shopping malls.

Part 4: Reading for Viewpoints (10 Questions)

Read the opinion article below and answer questions 1-10.

Title: Should Schools Start Later in the Morning?

Many experts argue that schools should start later in the morning, especially for teenagers who like to sleep in. Studies show that adolescents naturally fall asleep and wake up later, so early school start times can actually have a negative impact on their health and academic performance.

Starting school later can help students get more sleep, which in turn will lead to better concentration and fewer absences. It could even reduce the risk of depression and other mental health problems that are commonly found in teenagers.

However, some parents and teachers worry that changing start times could interfere with after-school activities and family schedules. Additionally, later dismissal times may affect part-time jobs and transportation arrangements.

Despite these concerns, several schools around the world have successfully implemented later start times, yielding positive results.

1. What is the main argument in favor of later school start times?

A) It helps students get more sleep.

B) It allows more time for homework.

C) It improves after-school activity participation.

D) It benefits parents' schedules.

2. What negative effects are linked to early start times?

A) Poor diet.

B) Mental health issues and poor concentration.

C) Increased social activity.

D) Transportation arrangements.

3. What is a concern of parents and teachers?

A) Students sleeping too much.

B) Difficulty scheduling after-school activities.

C) Higher costs for schools.

D) More homework load.

4. What impact could later dismissal times have?

A) Affect part-time jobs and transport.

B) Improve family meals.

C) Allow more study time.

D) Reduce traffic congestion.

5. What have schools that started later reported?

A) Negative academic results.

B) Increased student absenteeism.

C) Positive outcomes.

D) No changes at all.

6. Why do teenagers have later sleep patterns?

A) Because of homework.

B) Biological changes during adolescence.

C) Poor sleep habits.

D) Lack of exercise.

7. What mental health problem is mentioned?

A) Anxiety.

B) Depression.

C) Schizophrenia.

D) ADHD.

8. What is NOT a reason schools should start later?

A) To improve mental health.

B) To allow students to sleep more.

C) To match parents' schedules.

D) To improve concentration.

9. Who are the stakeholders mentioned?

A) Only students.

B) Students, parents, and teachers.

C) Teachers and doctors.

D) Parents only.

10. What is the author's tone?

A) Neutral.

B) Supportive of later start times.

C) Opposed to change.

D) Uncertain.

WRITING SECTION

Time: 53–60 minutes

Tasks: 2

Task 1: Writing an Email (27 minutes)

Scenario:

You recently stayed at a hotel and experienced some problems during your stay. Write an email to the hotel manager to explain the issues and suggest how they could improve the experience for future guests.

Requirements:

- Explain the problems you encountered.
- Describe how these issues affected your stay.
- Suggest ways the hotel could improve.
- Use appropriate tone and style for a formal email.

Word count: 150–200 words.

Task 2: Responding to Survey Question (26 minutes)

Scenario:

Your city council is planning to build a new park in your neighborhood. They have asked residents to share their opinions. Write a response explaining your opinion on the project.

Requirements:

- State whether you support or oppose the park project.
- Explain your reasons.
- Suggest what features you would like to see in the park (if you support it).
- Use a clear and friendly tone.

Word count: 150–200 words.

SPEAKING SECTION

Time: Approximately 15–20 minutes

Tasks: 8

Task 1: Giving Advice (1 minute preparation, 1–2 minutes response)

Question: A friend is feeling stressed about their upcoming exams. What advice would you give them?

Task 2: Talking about a Personal Experience (1 minute preparation, 1–2 minutes response)

Question: Describe a memorable vacation you had. What made it special?

Task 3: Describing a Scene (30-second preparation, 1-minute response)

Question: Look at the picture. Describe what you see.

https://www.pexels.com/photo/people-gathered-in-front-of-toronto-freestanding-signage-1750754/

Task 4: Making Predictions (30-second preparation, 1-minute response)

Question: What do you think will happen if more people start using electric cars?

Task 5: Comparing and Persuading (1 minute preparation, 1–2 minutes response)

Question: Compare living in the city with living in the countryside. Which do you prefer and why?

Task 6: Dealing with a Difficult Situation (1 minute preparation, 1–2 minutes response)

Question: Imagine you ordered food at a restaurant but received the wrong dish. How would you handle this situation?

Task 7: Expressing Opinions (1 minute preparation, 1–2 minutes response)

Question: Do you think technology has made our lives better or worse? Explain your opinion.

Task 8: Describing an Unusual Situation (1 minute preparation, 1–2 minutes response)

Question: Describe an unusual or surprising event you experienced. What happened?

Fred Winstone

CELPIP Mock Test 1 – Answers

Listening Section

Part 1: Listening to Problem Solving (8 Questions)

Answers:

1. B - Hiking
2. C - Stay in and read
3. B - Jason's kayak had a leak
4. C - Patched a leak
5. C - Sunscreen and snacks
6. B - 9 am
7. B - Saturday
8. C - Nice

Part 2: Listening to Daily Life Conversation (5 Questions)

Answers:

1. B - The coffee machine is broken
2. C - Three times
3. C - Replacing the coffee machine
4. B - One with a grinder
5. B - Write to the office manager

Part 3: Listening for Information (6 Questions)

Answers:

1. C - Remote work
2. C - Tech consultant
3. B - Better mental health
4. C - His business requires physical presence
5. C - She felt isolated from working at home
6. C - Trust their employees

Part 4: Listening to a News Item (5 Questions)

Answers:

1. B - A newly constructed pedestrian bridge
2. C - Over Highway 16
3. C - An example of community collaboration
4. C - To improve access to a park
5. C - A local runner

Part 5: Listening to a Discussion (8 Questions)

Answers:

1. C - World War I

2. C - Friday
3. B - Political causes and slides
4. B - Thursday morning
5. D - In the library
6. B - Leo
7. C - Research World War I battles
8. D - Have Leo's part ready to review

Part 6: Listening to Viewpoints (6 Questions)

Answers:

1. B - Whether it's okay to let go of old friendships
2. C - She believes friendships should feel mutual and real
3. A - That people don't take relationships seriously anymore
4. C - She appreciates them but doesn't want to force anything
5. D - They sometimes require showing up even when it's hard
6. B - Alia sees change as natural; Jacob values trying to maintain long-term connections

Reading Section

Part 1: Reading Correspondence

Answers:

1. A - To invite staff to a workshop
2. C - October 21st
3. C - Effective communication
4. C - Conference Room B
5. B - Confirm attendance by October 15th
6. B - Lunch and refreshments
7. B - HR Manager
8. B - Contact HR
9. C - The cost
10. D - Presentation skills and teamwork
11. A - Formal and enthusiastic

Part 2: Reading to Apply a Diagram or Map

Answers:

1. A - Near the entrance
2. D - Circulation Desk
3. C - Straight ahead
4. B - Near the entrance
5. A - Children's Section

6. C - Café

7. A - To borrow and return books

8. C - Study Rooms

Part 3: Reading for Information

Answers:

1. B - Growing plants in small city spaces

2. B - It provides fresh, organic food

3. B - By reducing food transport distances

4. C - Relieves stress

5. B - Bees and butterflies

6. B - They provide shade and cool down cities

7. B - Soil contamination

8. B - With planning and community support

9. B - Balconies, rooftops, and community gardens

Part 4: Reading For Viewpoints

Answers:

1. A - It helps students get more sleep

2. D - Transportation arrangements

3. B - Difficulty scheduling after-school activities

4. A - Affect part-time jobs and transport

5. C - Positive outcomes

6. B - Biological changes during adolescence

7. B - Depression

8. C - To match parents' schedules

9. B - Students, parents, and teachers

10. A - Neutral

Writing Section

Task 1: Writing an Email

Dear Hotel Manager,

I just returned home from a stay at your hotel and wanted to share some feedback. During my stay, I faced a few issues that affected my experience. The air conditioning in my room was not working, which made it extremely uncomfortable. The Wi-Fi connection was also unreliable, which made it difficult to work remotely.

These problems detracted from an otherwise pleasant stay. To improve, I suggest that you do regular maintenance checks on air conditioners and upgrade your internet infrastructure. Despite these concerns, I appreciated the helpful staff and the convenient location.

Thank you for your attention.

Sincerely,

[Your Name]

Task 2: Responding to Survey Questions

Dear City Council,

I support the plan to build a new park in our neighborhood. Parks allow families access to grass spaces and also allow people to enjoy outdoor activities, which promotes health and community relationships.

I hope the park will include walking trails, playgrounds, an outside gym, and picnic areas, as this will be a great addition for many residents. Additionally, creating more green spaces will help improve air quality and reduce the heat we feel in the city. I look forward to this positive addition to our community.

Thank you for considering residents' views.

Best regards,

[Your Name]

Speaking Section

(Sample model responses, approx. 1–2 minutes each)

Task 1: Giving Advice

I would advise my friend to make a study plan to organize their time and avoid last-minute stress.

Taking short breaks during study sessions helps maintain focus. I'd also remind them to get enough sleep and eat well to maintain their energy. Lastly, I'd encourage them to have a positive mindset and remind them that it's okay to ask for help.

Task 2: Talking about a Personal Experience

A memorable vacation I had was visiting the ocean last summer. The ocean breeze and dolphin sightings made it a special time for my family. The vacation really helped me to bond with my family, especially after a hard year.

Task 3: Describing a Scene

In the picture, I see a place in Toronto where people are ice-skating on an outdoor ice rink. There are also big buildings in the background. The scene is very busy, showing people out and about in the city having a good time.

Task 4: Making Predictions

If more people use electric cars, air pollution would decrease, which will make our cities a lot cleaner and promote better health for the residents. However, I believe that there are challenges, as the city would have to build more charging stations, and not everyone can afford an electric car.

Task 5: Comparing and Persuading

I prefer the countryside because it's peaceful and less crowded. The air is cleaner, and there is more nature. While the city has more job opportunities, shopping, and entertainment, the quiet environment of the countryside suits me better.

Task 6: Dealing with a Difficult Situation

I would politely tell the waiter about the mistake and ask if they could bring the dish I ordered. Usually, the staff are understanding and will correct the order quickly.

Task 7: Expressing Opinions

Technology has improved our lives by making communication easier and providing instant information. It helps with work and entertainment. However, it can sometimes be distracting, especially when it comes to children and teenagers, so it's important to use it wisely.

Task 8: Describing an Unusual Situation

Once, I was caught in a sudden rainstorm without an umbrella. A stranger shared theirs with me, and we walked together until the rain stopped. It was a kind, but unexpected gesture.

The CELPIP General Study Guide

CELPIP Mock Test 2 – Full Questions

LISTENING SECTION

Time: 46-55 minutes

Parts: 6

Total Questions: 38

Full Listening Test

Remember to only play the video once.

Part 1: Listening to Problem Solving (8 Questions)

Video Transcript: (Two roommates, Alex and Jordan, discuss an issue with their internet connection.)

Alex: Jordan, have you noticed the internet's been cutting out lately?

Jordan: Yeah, especially during the evenings. I couldn't even finish my video call with my mom last night.

Alex: I called the provider this morning. They said it might be the router. It's over five years old.

Jordan: That makes sense. Should we buy a new one?

Alex: I looked up a few options. We can get a decent one for under a hundred dollars. I can split the cost with you.

Jordan: Sure, that's fine. Can we get it today?

Alex: Yeah, there's one at TechMart. I'll go pick it up after work.

Jordan: Great. Hopefully, no more dropped connections!

Questions:

1. What problem are Alex and Jordan facing?
    - A. A broken television
    - B. Internet outages
    - C. Lost house keys
    - D. Late rent payments
2. When does the issue usually happen?
    - A. In the morning
    - B. At lunchtime
    - C. In the evenings
    - D. Overnight

3. Who did Alex call?
    - A. His mom
    - B. A technician
    - C. The internet provider
    - D. Jordan's workplace

4. How old is the router?
    - A. One year
    - B. Three years
    - C. Five years
    - D. Over five years

5. What does the provider suggest is the issue?
    - A. Poor weather
    - B. A power outage
    - C. The old router
    - D. Software updates

6. How much does Alex say the new router might cost?
    - A. Under $100
    - B. Over $200
    - C. Exactly $100
    - D. Less than $50

7. Who will pay for the router?

    o A. Alex
    o B. Jordan
    o C. Both of them
    o D. The provider

8. Where will Alex get the router?

    o A. Online store
    o B. TechMart
    o C. Supermarket
    o D. Electronics convention

Part 2: Listening to a Daily Life Conversation (5 Questions)

Video Transcript: (A father and daughter talking after school)

Daughter: Dad, we have a field trip next week to the science museum!

Father: That sounds exciting! Do you need to bring anything?

Daughter: Just a lunch and a signed permission slip. Can you sign it tonight?

Father: Of course. What day is the trip?

Daughter: Tuesday. We'll leave right after the morning bell.

Father: I went to that museum when I was your age. They had a big dinosaur skeleton.

Daughter: I hope it's still there!

Questions:

1. Where is the girl going for a field trip?
    - A. Art gallery
    - B. Zoo
    - C. Science Museum
    - D. Library

2. What does she need to bring?
    - A. A change of clothes
    - B. A camera
    - C. A lunch and permission slip
    - D. Her school books

3. What day is the field trip?
    - A. Monday
    - B. Tuesday
    - C. Wednesday
    - D. Friday

4. When will the class leave?
   - ○ A. After lunch
   - ○ B. After school
   - ○ C. Before the morning bell
   - ○ D. After the morning bell
5. What exhibit does the father remember?
   - ○ A. A space shuttle
   - ○ B. A robot
   - ○ C. A dinosaur skeleton
   - ○ D. An ancient mummy

Part 3: Listening for Information (6 Questions)

Video Transcript: (A recorded telephone conversation)

Caller: Hi, I'm calling about the ad for the apartment on Lakeside Avenue. Is it still available?

Agent: Yes, it is. It is a two-bedroom unit on the third floor, with a balcony and updated kitchen.

Caller: That sounds good. Is it close to public transportation?

Agent: Yes, actually, it's only a five-minute walk from the Green Line station, and there's a bus stop just around the corner.

Caller: Perfect. And what's the monthly rent?

Agent: It's $1,450, which includes water and heating. You'd just need to cover electricity and internet.

Caller: Okay. Are pets allowed?

Agent: Small pets, yes. There's a two-pet limit and a non-refundable pet deposit of $200.

Caller: Got it. I'd like to schedule a viewing. Is tomorrow afternoon possible?

Agent: Sure, we have a 2:30 pm slot open. I'll pencil you in.

Caller: Thanks, see you then.

Agent: Looking forward to it!

---

1. What is the caller inquiring about?

    A. A job opening

    B. A lost item

    C. An apartment for rent

    D. A cleaning service

2. What feature does the apartment include?

    A. A shared laundry room

    B. A balcony and modern kitchen

    C. Free internet and parking

    D. Three bedrooms and a backyard

3. How far is the apartment from the Green Line station?

    A. Two minutes by car

    B. Ten-minute walk

    C. Five-minute walk

    D. Right next to the station

4. What does the monthly rent not include?

    A. Water

    B. Heating

    C. Electricity

    D. Garbage collection

5. What is the building's pet policy?

    A. No pets allowed

    B. Only cats are allowed

    C. Pets are allowed with a refundable fee

D. Small pets allowed with a non-refundable deposit

6. What is the viewing scheduled?

   A. Tomorrow morning

   B. Tomorrow afternoon at 2:30

   C. This evening at 5:00

   D. Next week at noon

Part 4: Listening to News Item (5 Questions)

Video Transcript: (A news anchor reports on a new city recycling program)

News Anchor: The City of Brookhaven launched a new recycling initiative this Monday aimed at reducing household waste. Under the new program, residents will receive color-coded bins for paper, plastic, and glass. The initiative also includes educational workshops on sustainable living.

City spokesperson Carla Mendes says the goal is to reduce landfill contributions by 30% over the next year. Residents are encouraged to attend the workshop sessions at community centers throughout the month.

Local resident David Tran, who participated in the pilot program last year, says it's easy to follow and helps families become more environmentally conscious.

Questions:

1. What is the news item about?

    o   A. Road construction

    o   B. A recycling program

    o   C. A city garden project

    o   D. Water restrictions

2. What do residents receive under the program?

    o   A. A compost bin

    o   B. Recycling posters

    o   C. Color-coded bins

    o   D. Trash coupons

3. What is included in the initiative?

    o   A. Tree planting

    o   B. Recycling contests

    o   C. Educational workshops

    o   D. Street cleaning

4. What is the city's goal for landfill reduction?

    o A. 10%

    o B. 20%

    o C. 25%

    o D. 30%

5. Where are workshops being held?

    o A. Schools

    o B. Libraries

    o C. Community centers

    o D. Government offices

Part 5: Listening to a Discussion (8 Questions)

Video Transcript: (Colleagues Olivia and Mark talk about planning an office charity event)

Olivia: Mark, have you thought about which charity we should support for the office fundraiser?

Mark: I was thinking of the local food bank. They've had a surge in demand lately.

Olivia: That's a great idea. Should we do a silent auction again?

Mark: Maybe something new. How about a trivia night?

Olivia: I love that! We could have teams from each department.

Mark: Perfect. Let's book the cafeteria and send out invites by Friday.

Questions:
1. What are Olivia and Mark planning?
    - A. A staff meeting
    - B. A birthday party
    - C. A charity event
    - D. A training session
2. Which organization do they want to support?
    - A. Animal shelter
    - B. Local library
    - C. Food bank
    - D. Hospital
3. What activity do they decide on?
    - A. Silent auction
    - B. Trivia night
    - C. Bake sale
    - D. Marathon

4. Who will participate in the event?
   - ○ A. Customers
   - ○ B. Students
   - ○ C. Staff teams
   - ○ D. Board members

5. What is the deadline for sending invites?
   - ○ A. Wednesday
   - ○ B. Thursday
   - ○ C. Friday
   - ○ D. Monday

6. Why does Mark suggest the food bank?
   - ○ A. They sponsored a recent event
   - ○ B. They are struggling financially
   - ○ C. There's been a rise in need
   - ○ D. It was Olivia's first choice

7. What location do they plan to use?
   - ○ A. Main office
   - ○ B. Cafeteria
   - ○ C. Outdoor garden
   - ○ D. Break room

8. What did they do in the past for fundraising?
   - A. Trivia night
   - B. Raffle draw
   - C. Silent auction
   - D. Talent show

Part 6: Listening to Viewpoints (6 Questions)

Video Transcript: (A podcast interview with two guests discussing electric cars)

Host: Today on EcoTalk, we're diving into the pros and cons of electric vehicles. With me are Clara, an environmental policy researcher, and Dan, an automotive mechanic.

Clara: Thanks for having me. I think EVs are essential for reducing emissions. They're quieter and cleaner overall.

Dan: I agree to some extent, but I see a lot of EVs coming in with battery issues. Replacing those batteries is expensive and not very eco-friendly either.

Clara: That's true, but technology is improving. Governments are also offering incentives to make EVs more accessible.

Dan: Incentives help, but charging infrastructure still needs work, especially in rural areas.

Clara: Absolutely. More investment in public charging is key.

Host: Sounds like there's progress, but also some challenges ahead.

Questions:

1. What is the topic of the discussion?
    - A. Fuel prices
    - B. Electric vehicles
    - C. Public transit
    - D. Car insurance
2. What does Clara say is a benefit of EVs?
    - A. Lower fuel tax
    - B. Cleaner and quieter
    - C. Better resale value
    - D. Longer range
3. What issue does Dan bring up?
    - A. Poor mileage
    - B. Lack of style
    - C. Battery problems
    - D. Noise levels

4. Why are battery replacements a concern?

    o   A. They're unavailable

    o   B. They're slow to install

    o   C. They're expensive and harmful

    o   D. They void warranties

5. What does Clara say about battery technology?

    o   A. It's getting worse

    o   B. It's too complex

    o   C. It's improving

    o   D. It's no longer a problem

6. What incentive do governments offer?

    o   A. Free parking

    o   B. Charging vouchers

    o   C. Purchase rebates

    o   D. Extra warranty

READING SECTION

Time: 43-56 minutes

Parts: 4

Total Questions: 38

Part 1: Reading Correspondence (11 questions)

Read the email below and answer questions 1-10.

Subject: Invitation to Community Clean-Up Day

Dear Neighbors,

We are excited to invite you to our annual Community Clean-Up Day on Saturday, July 15th. Volunteers are scheduled to gather at the community center at 9:00 am and will be given gloves, bags, and some refreshments.

This event is a wonderful opportunity to help keep our neighborhood clean and meet new people. Please bring comfortable shoes and dress for the weather.

If you would like to volunteer, kindly reply to this email by July 1st. We hope to see many of you there!

Best regards,

The Neighborhood Association

Questions:

1. **When is the Community Clean-Up Day?**
   - A. July 1st
   - B. July 9th
   - C. July 15th
   - D. July 25th

2. **Where will volunteers meet?**
   - A. Local Park
   - B. Neighborhood Association office
   - C. Town hall
   - D. Community center

3. **What will volunteers receive?**
   - A. T-shirts and shoes
   - B. Gloves, bags, and refreshments
   - C. Money and food vouchers
   - D. Gift cards and maps

4. **What should volunteers bring?**
   - A. Sunscreen and snacks
   - B. Umbrellas and bottled water
   - C. Comfortable shoes and weather-appropriate clothing
   - D. Their own trash bags

5. **How can residents volunteer?**
    - A. Call the mayor's office
    - B. Fill out a paper form
    - C. Reply to the email
    - D. Visit the website

6. **Who is organizing the event?**
    - A. City Council
    - B. Local school board
    - C. The Neighborhood Association
    - D. Volunteer Services

7. **What is the main purpose of the event?**
    - A. Raise money for charity
    - B. Celebrate a holiday
    - C. Clean up the neighborhood
    - D. Provide job training

8. **What time does the event start?**
    - A. 8:00 am.
    - B. 9:00 am.
    - C. 10:00 am.
    - D. Noon

9. **By what date should volunteers respond?**

    ○ A. June 30th

    ○ B. July 1st

    ○ C. July 5th

    ○ D. July 15th

10. **What is included to keep volunteers comfortable?**

    ○ A. Tents and water bottles

    ○ B. Breakfast and lunch

    ○ C. Gloves, bags, and refreshments

    ○ D. Sunscreen and fans

11. **What tone does the email use?**

    ○ A. Critical and urgent

    ○ B. Formal and distant

    ○ C. Friendly and encouraging

    ○ D. Informative and apologetic

Part2: Reading to Apply a Diagram (8 questions)

Refer to the pie chart below and answer questions 1-8.

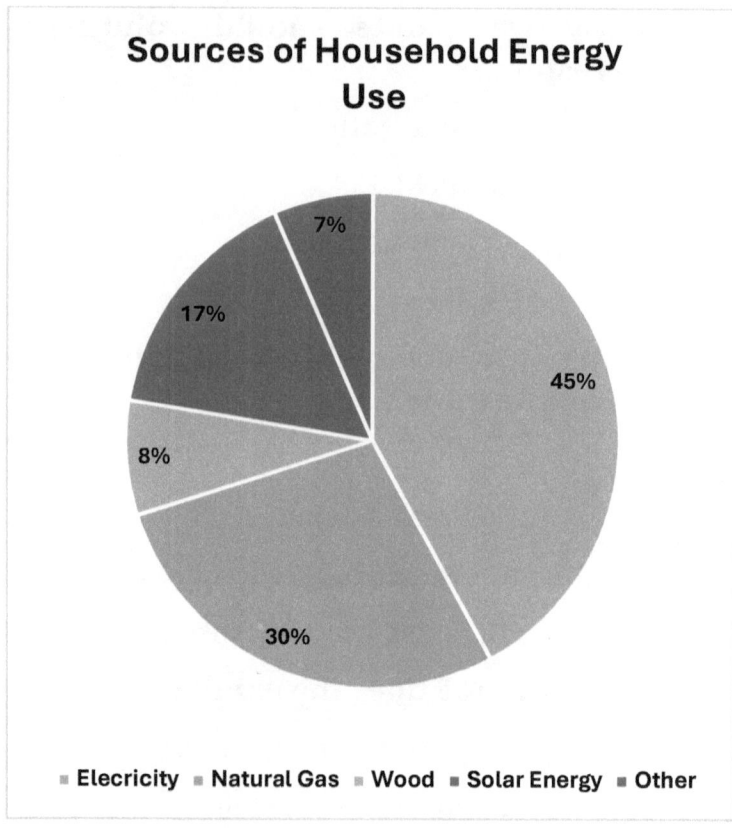

Pie Chart: Sources of Household Energy Use

- **Electricity:** 45%
- **Natural Gas:** 30%
- **Wood:** 8%
- **Solar Energy:** 17%
- **Other:** 7%

Questions:

1. **Which energy source is used the most?**

    o A. Solar Energy

    o B. Natural Gas

    o C. Electricity

    o D. Wood

2. **What percentage of energy use is natural gas?**

    o A. 25%

    o B. 30%

    o C. 35%

    o D. 40%

3. **How much more is electricity used than solar energy?**

    o A. 35%

    o B. 20%

    o C. 25%

    o D. 15%

4. **Which source is least used?**

    o A. Solar Energy

    o B. Other

- C. Wood
- D. Natural Gas

5. **How many categories are shown?**
   - A. 4
   - B. 5
   - C. 6
   - D. 3

6. **What portion of energy comes from renewable sources (solar and wood)?**
   - A. 10%
   - B. 15%
   - C. 18%
   - D. 25%

7. **Is natural gas used more than electricity?**
   - A. Yes
   - B. No
   - C. They are equal
   - D. Not stated

8. **What percentage is labeled as 'Other'?**
   - A. 5%

- B. 6%
- C. 7%
- D. 8%

Part 3: Reading for Information (9 questions)

Read the advertisement below and answer questions 1-9.

Explore Downtown Art Gallery

The Downtown Art Gallery is hosting an exhibition of local artists from August 1st to August 31st. The gallery is open Tuesday to Sunday from 10:00 am to 6:00 pm. Admission is free.

Special events during the exhibition include artist talks every Saturday at 2:00 pm and workshops on Sunday afternoons. Parking is available behind the gallery.

Visit our website for more details.

Questions:

1. **When is the exhibition running?**
    - A. July 1st to July 31st
    - B. August 1st to August 31st

- C. September 1st to September 30th
- D. August 15th to September 15th

2. **What are the gallery's opening days?**
    - A. Monday to Friday
    - B. Tuesday to Sunday
    - C. Every day
    - D. Weekends only

3. **What time does the gallery close?**
    - A. 5:00 pm.
    - B. 6:00 pm.
    - C. 7:00 pm.
    - D. 8:00 pm.

4. **Is there an admission fee?**
    - A. Yes, $10
    - B. Yes, $5
    - C. No, it is free
    - D. Only for special events

5. **When are the artist talks?**
    - A. Fridays at 2:00 pm.
    - B. Saturdays at 2:00 pm.
    - C. Sundays at 2:00 pm.

- D. Mondays at 2:00 pm.

6. **What can visitors do on Sunday afternoons?**
    - A. Attend workshops
    - B. Watch movies
    - C. Take guided tours
    - D. Buy art supplies

7. **Where can visitors park?**
    - A. On the street in front of the gallery
    - B. In a parking garage downtown
    - C. Behind the gallery
    - D. At a nearby shopping mall

8. **Where can more information be found?**
    - A. At the gallery's entrance
    - B. In local newspapers
    - C. On the gallery's website
    - D. By calling the city hall

9. **What kind of artists are featured?**
    - A. International artists
    - B. Local artists

- C. Student artists
- D. Famous artists from the past

Part 4: Reading for Viewpoints (10 questions)

Read the letter to the editor and answer questions 1-10.

Subject: Opinion on City's Recycling Program

Dear Editor,

I appreciate the city's efforts to improve recycling, but I believe more needs to be done. Many residents are confused about what materials can be recycled, and collection schedules are extremely inconsistent.

Clearer instructions on recycling bins and a more reliable pick-up timetable would help people to participate more. Additionally, educational programs in schools could raise awareness among children.

I hope the city will take these suggestions into consideration to make the recycling program more effective.

Sincerely,

A Concerned Resident

Questions:

1. **What is the main concern of the writer?**

    A. Lack of recycling bins

    B. Confusion about recycling and collection issues

    C. High recycling fees

    D. Too many recycling locations

2. **What problem do residents face?**

    A. Recycling bins are too small

    B. Collection schedules are inconsistent

    C. No recycling program exists

    D. Recycling is mandatory

3. **What does the writer suggest about collection schedules?**

    A. They should be shorter

    B. They need to be more reliable

    C. They should be less frequent

    D. They are fine as they are

4. **What could help increase participation?**

    A. Clearer instructions and reliable pick-up times

    B. Fines for not recycling

    C. More recycling trucks

    D. Free recycling bags

5. **Who should be targeted by educational programs?**

    A. Seniors

    B. Business owners

    C. Children in schools

    D. Tourists

6. **What does the writer appreciate?**

    A. The city's efforts to improve recycling

    B. Free recycling bins

    C. Lower taxes

    D. More parks

7. **What is the tone of the letter?**

    A. Angry and aggressive

    B. Supportive but critical

    C. Indifferent

    D. Humorous

8. **What does the writer hope the city will do?**

    A. Cancel the recycling program

    B. Consider the suggestions to improve the program

    C. Increase recycling fees

    D. Hire more employees

9. **Which of the following is NOT mentioned as a suggestion?**

    A. Clearer instructions on bins

    B. Educational programs in schools

    C. Fines for non-recyclers

    D. More reliable pick-up timetable

10. **What is the writer's relationship to the city?**

    A. A city official

    B. A concerned resident

    C. A recycling worker

    D. A business owner

WRITING SECTION

Time: 53 minutes

Parts: 2

Task 1: Writing an Email (Write an email based on the prompt)

You recently stayed at a local gym and want to give feedback. Write an email to the gym manager explaining what you liked and what could be improved. Include at least two positives and two suggestions for improvement.

Task 2: Responding to Survey Questions (Write a response to a survey question)

Your city is considering adding bike lanes on major roads. Do you support or oppose this idea? Explain your opinion and give reasons for your answer.

SPEAKING SECTION

Time: 15 minutes

Parts: 8

Task 1: Giving Advice

Your friend is nervous about a job interview. What advice would you give them to help them prepare?

Task 2: Talking about a Personal Experience

Describe a memorable event from your childhood. Explain why it was memorable.

Task 3: Describing a Scene

Look at the picture of a busy call center below and describe what you see.

https://www.pexels.com/photo/people-in-cubicles-of-call-center-5453859/

Task 4: Making Predictions

Predict what changes technology will bring to education in the next 10 years.

Task 5: Comparing and Persuading

Compare living in a city versus living in a small town. Which do you prefer and why?

Task 6: Dealing with a Difficult Situation

Imagine your child's teacher called you to let you know that your child has been behaving badly. What would you do?

Task 7: Expressing Opinions

Do you think people should work from home? Why or why not?

Task 8: Describing an Unusual Situation

Describe an unusual or surprising experience you have had.

_____

_____

Fred Winstone

CELPIP Mock Test 2 – Answers

Listening Section

Part 1: Listening to Problem Solving (8 Questions)

1. B - Internet outages
2. C - In the evenings
3. C - The internet provider
4. D - Over five years
5. C - The old router
6. C - Less than $50
7. C - Both of them
8. B - Electronics convention

Part 2: Listening to a Daily Life Conversation (5 Questions)

1. C - Science Museum
2. C - A lunch and permission slip
3. B - Tuesday
4. D - After the morning bell
5. C - A dinosaur skeleton

Part 3: Listening for Information (6 Questions)

1. C - An apartment for rent
2. B - A balcony and modern kitchen
3. C - Five-minute walk
4. C - Electricity
5. D - Small pets allowed with a non-refundable deposit
6. B - Tomorrow afternoon at 2:30

Part 4: Listening to a News Item (5 Questions)

1. B - A recycling program
2. C - Color-coded bins
3. C - Educational workshops
4. D - 30%
5. C - Community centers

Part 5: Listening to a Discussion (8 Questions)

1. C - A charity event
2. C - Food bank
3. B - Trivia night
4. C - Staff teams
5. C - Friday

6. C - There's been a rise in need
7. B - Cafeteria
8. C - Silent auction

Part 6: Listening to Viewpoints (6 Questions)

1. B - Electric vehicles
2. B - Cleaner and quieter
3. C - Battery problems
4. C - They're expensive and harmful
5. C - It's improving
6. C - Purchase rebates

Reading Section Answers

Part 1: Reading Correspondence (11 Questions)

1. C - July 15th
2. D - Community center
3. B - Gloves, bags, and refreshments
4. C - Comfortable shoes and weather-appropriate clothing
5. C - Reply to the email
6. C - The Neighborhood Association

7. C - Clean up the neighborhood
8. B - 9:00 am.
9. B - July 1st
10. C - Gloves, bags, and refreshments
11. C - Friendly and encouraging

Part 2: Reading to Apply a Diagram (8 Questions)

1. C - Electricity
2. B - 30%
3. A - 35%
4. B - Other
5. B - 5
6. C - 18%
7. B - No
8. C - 7%

Part 3: Reading for Information (9 Questions)

1. B - August 1st to August 31st
2. B - Tuesday to Sunday
3. B - 6:00 pm.
4. C - No, it is free
5. B - Saturdays at 2:00 pm.

6. A - Attend workshops
7. C - Behind the gallery
8. C - On the gallery's website
9. B - Local artists

Part 3: Reading Viewpoints (10 Questions)

1. B - Confusion about recycling and collection issues
2. B - Collection schedules are inconsistent
3. B - They need to be more reliable
4. A - Clearer instructions and reliable pick-up times
5. C - Children in schools
6. A - Lower taxes
7. B - Supportive but critical
8. B - Supportive but critical
9. C - Fines for non-recyclers
10. B - A concerned resident

Writing Section – Model Answers (Sample)

Task 1: Writing an Email

Dear Gym Manager,

I recently used your gym facilities and wanted to share my feedback. I really appreciated the clean equipment and friendly staff, which made my workouts enjoyable. However, I noticed that some machines were out of order, and the locker rooms could use better ventilation, as it was extremely hot inside. Improving these areas would make visits more comfortable. Overall, I had a positive experience and look forward to seeing these improvements.

Thank you for your attention.

Best regards,

[Your Name]

Task 2: Responding to Survey Questions

I support adding bike lanes on major roads in our city. Bike lanes make cycling safer by separating bikes from cars, which encourages more people to cycle. This can greatly reduce traffic congestion and pollution by improving the quality of the air. Additionally, bike lanes promote healthier lifestyles by encouraging physical activity. While some roads may need modifications to ensure the utmost safety, the long-term benefits for the environment and community far outweigh the challenges. Overall, bike lanes are a positive step towards a more sustainable and active city.

Speaking Section – Sample Responses (Brief Examples)

Task 1: Giving Advice

I would tell my friend to research the company, practice common interview questions, dress professionally, and get a good night's sleep before the interview. I would also advise them to have a sustainable breakfast and remind them that being prepared can help them calm their nerves.

Task 2: Talking about a Personal Experience

One memorable event was my school's sports day. I won a race, which made me feel very proud. It was memorable because I trained hard and felt great winning the race and getting a trophy in front of my friends and family.

Task 3: Describing a Scene

In the busy call center, I see many office partitions where people are on the phone with customers. Some employees are chatting, while others look bored. One employee looks frustrated, as he is holding his eyes closed. The atmosphere seems busy and stressful, yet productive.

Task 4: Making Predictions

In the next 10 years, technology will make education more interactive with virtual reality and online classes. Students will be able to learn at their own pace, and teachers will have more tools to support different and effective learning styles.

Task 5: Comparing and Persuading

Living in a city offers convenience like shops and public transit, but it's noisy and crowded. A small town is quieter and safer, but fewer activities are available. I prefer a small town because of its peaceful environment.

Task 6: Dealing with a Difficult Situation

If my child's teacher contacted me to say that my child was misbehaving at school, I would politely tell her that I would speak with my child when I got home from work. I would ask them to talk about it and tell them not to behave like that again.

Task 7: Expressing Opinions

I think working from home is good because it saves commute time and offers flexibility. However, some people might miss social interaction with coworkers, and battle to be productive if their home workspace is not set up correctly.

Task 8: Describing an Unusual Situation

Once I saw my cat and dog cuddling up to each other on a cold winter's day. It was surprising, as they normally do not get along very well, so I did not expect to see this.

Scoring Guide Summary – What Makes These Good Responses?

- **Listening & Reading**: Pay attention to key facts, tone, and speaker intention. Many answers require *inference* rather than exact repetition.
- **Writing**:
    - Use **a clear structure**: introduction, body, conclusion.
    - Write in **complete sentences** with proper punctuation.

- o Use **transition words** (Firstly, Secondly, Therefore...).
- **Speaking**:
  - o Speak **clearly and confidently**.
  - o Use **details and examples** to support your answers.
  - o Avoid long pauses. Practice helps!

Great job finishing these two full-length CELPIP practice tests! Practicing like this really helps you get comfortable with the format and timing, so you won't be caught off guard on test day. Take some time to go over the model answers and scoring tips, as these will show you where you're doing well and what you can work on next.

Keep practicing a little every day, and you'll see your confidence grow. Remember, it's all about steady progress. Keep going and good luck with your CELPIP journey!

Wishing you all the best on your new Canadian adventure!

Conclusion

You've reached the final chapter, and that alone is a reason to feel proud! Preparing for the CELPIP – General Test takes time, energy, and a lot of focus. Whether you're doing this for immigration, career opportunities, or personal achievement, the fact that you've taken this step shows just how committed you are to your goals.

Let's take a moment to reflect on what this book was really all about. Essentially, this wasn't just about passing a test. It was about helping you communicate clearly, confidently, and naturally in English. The test is designed to measure how well you use English in real-life situations, and that's exactly what we've focused on throughout these pages.

A Quick Recap of the Journey

We started with the basics—what the CELPIP test is, why it matters, and how it's structured. Then we broke it down, section by section:

- In the **Listening Test**, we looked at how to stay focused, identify tone and purpose, and listen for key information even under time pressure.

- The **Reading Test** taught us how to skim, scan, and dig into the meaning of texts—skills that come in handy far beyond the exam.

- With the **Writing Test**, we explored how to organize ideas, express opinions, and build solid responses that are logical, clear, and well-supported.

- And in the **Speaking Test**, we talked about speaking naturally, thinking on your feet, and structuring your answers so your thoughts shine through.

Along the way, we also covered time management strategies, self-review tips, mindset techniques, and how to build habits that will keep your English strong well beyond test day.

At the beginning of this book, we made a promise. To help you feel fully prepared and confident walking into the CELPIP exam room. Now that you've worked through everything, you should feel a growing confidence. You now have a plan and the tools to make it happen.

The Big Takeaway: Progress Over Perfection

If there's one message to carry with you from this book, let it be this: **You don't need to be perfect. You just need to show what you know.**

CELPIP doesn't reward fancy words or robotic answers—it rewards natural communication. So, focus on being clear. Be calm. Be yourself. You've already taken so many steps toward success. Now it's time to bring that preparation to life.

Your Test Day Checklist

Feeling ready is about more than just knowledge; it's also about being organized. Here's a quick checklist to make sure test day goes smoothly:

Bring Your Valid ID	The same identification you used to register—make sure it's original, not expired, and not a copy.
Arrive Early	Arrive at least **45 minutes** before your scheduled time to complete check-in and relax before the test begins.
Leave Personal Items Behind	Phones, bags, notes, and other personal items are not allowed in the test room. Lockers are usually provided.
Use the Washroom Before the Test	Breaks are limited and controlled—use the restroom before you're called in.

Listen to Instructions	The proctor will walk you through the process. Listen carefully and follow directions closely.
Stay Calm	If you start to feel anxious, take a few slow breaths, remind yourself of your preparation, and stay focused.
Check the Official Site	For the most up-to-date details, always refer to the official CELPIP test-day page: https://www.celpip.ca/take-celpip/test-day-information/

Keep Growing: Your English Journey Doesn't Stop Here

Whether or not English is your first language, language learning is a journey that never truly ends. Here are some additional **resources** that may prove to be very helpful when building your skills and confidence:

Books

- *CELPIP Study Guide* by Paragon Testing
- *English Grammar in Use* by Raymond Murphy
- *The Elements of Style* by Strunk & White (for writing polish)

- *Fluent English* by Barbara Raifsnider

Websites & Blogs

- www.celpip.ca – Official site with webinars, free practice, and updates
- UsingEnglish.com – For grammar explanations and practice
- FluentU.com – Watch real-world English videos for listening practice
- IELTS Liz – Great writing and speaking tips that also apply to CELPIP

Twitter Accounts to Follow

- @celpiptest – The official CELPIP account
- @EnglishTips4U – Daily English learning tips
- @CambridgeWords – Vocabulary trends and grammar insights

A Final Word of Encouragement

Preparing for a big test like CELPIP can feel overwhelming at times. But please remember this: **you've already done the hard part**. You've committed to your goal. You've studied, practiced, learned, and grown. Test day is simply your opportunity to show everything you've worked so hard to develop.

You are ready. Truly.

Speak from your heart. Write with clarity. Read with focus. Listen carefully. You've got all the tools you need—now trust yourself to use them.

And if you ever feel nervous, just remind yourself: this test isn't a judgment. It's a reflection of your communication skills—and you've come a long way.

Thank You.... And One Last Favor

Thank you so much for choosing this book to support your preparation. It means a lot to us, and we truly hope it made your study experience clearer, calmer, and even enjoyable.

If this guide helped you feel more confident, focused, or prepared in any way, we'd be incredibly grateful if you could take a moment to leave a **5-star review on Amazon**. Your review helps other learners find a resource they can trust and helps us continue to improve and support others on this journey.

Let's Stay Connected

We'd love to hear how your test goes! You can find bonus content, updates, and even occasional live Q&A sessions through our website and newsletter. And if you've got questions, feedback, or even a success story—reach out! We're cheering for you.

So, here's to you!

Go take that test. Walk into that room with your head high, your thoughts clear, and your English skills ready to shine.

You've done the work. Now go show what you can do.

You've got this. Good luck!

**Yours,
Fred Winstone.**

www.ingramcontent.com/pod-product-compliance
Lightning Source LLC
Chambersburg PA
CBHW020403080526
44584CB00014B/1153